DATE DUE

Bureaucratic
Power
in
Society

Bureaucratic Power in Society

Richard Chackerian
and Gilbert Abcarian
Florida State University

Nelson-Hall nh Chicago

LIBRARY OF CONGRESS CATALOGING IN PUBLICATION DATA

Chackerian, Richard.
  Bureaucratic power in society.

  Bibliography: p.
  Includes index.
  1. Power (Social sciences) 2. Bureaucracy. 3. Social
exchange. I. Abcarian, Gilbert, 1925-   . II. Title.
HM271.C465 1984   303.3   83-17267
ISBN 0-8304-1004-X (cloth)
ISBN 0-8304-1116-X (paper)

Manufactured in the United States of America

10 9 8 7 6 5 4 3 2 1

The paper in this book is pH neutral (acid-free).

For our mothers:
Helen A. Chackerian
and Annie Abcarian

Contents

1

Bureaucratic Power and Personal Development

TODAY, THERE IS a crisis of trust in governmental and corporate institutions. There is an erosion of confidence in their technical competence, in their public responsiveness, and in their ability to regulate and control. It is thus hardly surprising that some writers, such as Harvey Wheeler, consider *bureaucracy* a term of ill repute. Bureaucracy, he says, is "a vast organism with an assortment of specialized, departmentalized tentacles for coping with the different kinds of reality it may encounter." The imagery suggested by "tentacles" is doubtless satisfying to those who perceive bureaucracy as an alien force that lurks everywhere and seeks to swallow everything that is creative, unroutinized, inefficient, spontaneous, or innovative.

Wheeler's implied criticism of bureaucracy seems tame compared to the passionate and dramatic language of Charles Reich:

> Beginning with school, if not before, an individual is systematically stripped of his imagination, his creativity, his heritage, his dreams, and his personal uniqueness, in order to style him into a productive unit for a mass, technological society. Instinct, feeling, and spontaneity are repressed by overwhelming forces. As the individual is drawn into the meritocracy, his working life is split from his homelife, and both suffer from a lack of wholeness. Eventually, people virtually become their profession, roles, or occupations and are therefore strangers to themselves.[2]

The statement may be misleading, however, because it implies that bureaucracy is an alien rather than a normal feature of society's social structure. It may be misleading also in implying that bureaucracy and meritocracy are forces of evil arrayed against individuals who seek growth as members of the family, school, or polity. Indeed, we shall see that bureaucratic power is, in some respects, indistinguishable from some of these cherished social institutions.

Others take bureaucracy for granted, regarding it as a force peripheral to their own central life problems and opportunities, something remote, impersonal, and vaguely necessary. It is seen as an organizational servant of the people, attending to its own rather technical internal concerns, and therefore essentially nonpolitical in mood and action, though quite useful. Crozier approaches this position:

> Young people will eventually have to discover, as some of us did in the fifties, that organizational life has some advantages for us imperfect human beings.... [O]rganizational life—the life that puts us in our little boxes—remains a relatively cheap and efficient way of providing us with the limits we need in order to play the games we like: games of conflict and cooperation, which we do not have to risk too much for ourselves or for our partners.[3]

Because bureaucracy serves important human interests, simple positive or negative evaluations of it are not very useful. The evaluation of bureaucracy in society is made complex by the fact that bureaucracy involves not only the formal organization of government and business but also various social institutions that are shaped by and help promote bureaucratic values and power. This point is central to the purpose of the book and we want to be clear about it: bureaucracy, we are saying, is found wherever such bureaucratic values as hierarchy, impersonality, and expertise are supported. This means that a wide variety of social roles can express the bureaucratic values that underlie bureaucratic power. Some of these values are found in work institutions; others are found in nonwork institutions such as the family, school, and political system.

A special concern of ours is with the web of relationships involving bureaucratized work institutions on the one hand, and the family, school, and political system on the other. The latter institutions are central because they provide the major avenues through which self-development is facilitated or hindered. Each of these institutions may have a profound impact on one's level of personal development. Therefore, we shall focus on the process by which the norms and values of bureaucratic work organization are diffused to individuals and affect opportunities for personal development.

The direct diffusion of bureaucratic values to workers is enormously important for the paths taken to personal development. Our approach emphasizes the indirect routes by which individuals adopt bureaucratic values. The indirect method calls attention to the ways in which primary institutions such as the family, school, and polity are influenced and transformed by bureaucratic power and how these reshaped primary institutions affect individuals. Bureaucratic power is "in" society in the sense that primary institutions are transformed by it.

Our concept of personal development is drawn from the work of the late humanistic psychologist Abraham H. Maslow. Maslow sees personal development as "self-actualization" and offers the following seminal definition:

> We may define self-actualization as an episode, or a spurt in
> which the powers of the person come together in a particularly
> efficient and intensely enjoyable way, and in which he is more
> integrated and less split.... He becomes in these episodes more
> truly himself, more perfectly actualizing his potentialities,
> closer to the core of his being, more fully human.[4]

The idea of self-actualization is not to be taken literally, but it
does suggest the importance of institutional arrangements that
encourage the integration of skills, abilities, sentiments, and
needs. The concept also emphasizes the developmental potential of all persons and the extent to which institutions encourage
or discourage that potential.

A major goal in succeeding chapters is to trace the relevance
and complexity of bureaucratic power for the primary institutions of family, school, and polity. We shall also explore the
ways in which bureaucratic values provide opportunities and
impose limits on the capacity of individuals to develop. We
regard such development as vital and socially constructive, and
therefore accept the constellation of moral and social values
that constitute preconditions for the ideal of personal development. All this we shall identify and examine in due course.

The capacity of individuals to develop or self-actualize
depends at least in part on having power. Power is necessary
because development requires (1) a capacity to set goals consistent with one's personal interests, skills, and aspirations, and
(2) control over the resources necessary for the attainment of
these goals. By power we mean the capacity of an individual or
group to induce others to comply through rewards for doing
so.[5] The emphasis here is on power based on rewards and values
rather than on the deterrent effect of force, a distinction
discussed below.

SOCIAL LIFE

Power and personal development have their roots in social
life. This means that power and personal development are con-

tingent on the actions of others. The satisfaction of basic needs such as love, security, and esteem involve social relationships between two or more individuals. We may characterize these social relationships in two distinct ways: those that are intrinsically gratifying, and those that tend to be pursued because of their instrumental value. Intrinsic relationships are valued not because some material benefit follows from the relationship but because the relationship as such is valued.

The distinction between intrinsic and instrumental relationships is important because satisfaction of a need for love and esteem can only result from intrinsic relationships. Ideally conceived, love implies an open-ended commitment and cannot survive when it depends on highly specialized contributions such as money, sex, intellectual stimulation, or companionship. It is difficult to be treated as a means to specialized ends and at the same time regard a relationship as satisfying one's need for love. Why then, assuming an awareness of personal intrinsic needs, are instrumental relationships accepted? Very simply because instrumental relationships are also fundamental and necessary. Instrumental relationships are necessary because basic material needs such as shelter and food are prerequisites of survival.

Types of rewards and social relationships cannot be neatly compartmentalized. In actuality, intrinsic and instrumental interactions provide the opportunity for the development of one another. For example, two students may be drawn to one another because of mutual admiration, each enjoying the intrinsic satisfaction of the relationship. Later, this intrinsically satisfying relationship may develop into an instrumental exchange of academic skills. The idealized nuclear family is a context in which intrinsic satisfactions are paramount. But family relationships also provide food, shelter, and economic support. Siblings cooperate in real estate ventures, parents and children become business partners, husbands and wives divide the task of providing income. Thus the intrinsic satisfaction of family ties are a condition for the exchange of extrinsic benefits.

Conversely, persons drawn together by the prospect of sharing instrumental benefits may develop intrinsically satisfying relationships as well. In preindustrial society, marriages were often economic contracts between families, with specific economic rights and obligations assigned to contracting families. Once the bargain had been made, loving relationships might then develop.

The mixing of intrinsic and extrinsic relationships in social institutions may be disruptive. Intrinsic values central to the major function of an institution are displaced by subsidiary instrumental values. The problem can be cast in the form of a question: What would a family look like and what consequences would follow for its members if its values and relationships were wholly instrumental in character? Conversely, what would a bureaucratic organization look like and what consequences would follow for its members if its values and relationships were wholly intrinsic? Our own premise in this matter should be clear. In both cases, individuals would be wholly unable to meet either their needs for gratification or their need for material support. From our perspective, a primary problem is to examine the conditions under which instrumental relationships diffuse to and dominate not only bureaucratic organizations but also the family, school, and political system.

POWER AS A CONSEQUENCE OF
EXCHANGE RELATIONSHIPS

Assessment of the conditions under which different types of values dominate requires careful consideration of how power becomes differentiated in social and institutional life. It was suggested above that power is the capacity to induce others to accede to one's wishes through the allocation of values and rewards. Power involves a relationship between the giver and the receiver of a benefit. The giver, however, does not have power over the receiver solely because of a unilateral gift. The receiver of the gift may simply take the reward and fail to reciprocate. But doing this means an end to the relationship. Given the norm of reciprocity in our culture, ingratitude will be "rewarded" by a discontinuance of benefits and thus a termination of the relationship. Ingratitude is likely to be expressed when the receiver does not prize the benefit or when it is felt that the benefit can be gotten elsewhere. Even if the benefits deriving from the relationship are important and cannot be gotten elsewhere, one need not become relatively powerless. If one possesses resources that are valued by the bestower of benefits, a relationship can be developed in which benefits are exchanged. Equality of control or power exists in this situation because each has a resource that is valued by the other.

A situation may arise when one needs the help of another but has nothing to exchange in return. The alternatives of the person who needs services are to seek help from another source, force another to give help, or get along without the help. If unwilling to choose any of these, the only remaining alternative is subordination to the giver, thereby rewarding him or her with power over oneself. This subordination may be "cashed-in" by the giver at a future time for undefined benefits.[6]

Rewarding others with power over oneself is the customary experience of many workers in large organizations. Workers are dependent on employers because the latter provide wages and benefits. This dependence is particularly great if workers are not willing to resort to force, if they have few alternatives to their current employment, or if they feel they cannot do without the wages and benefits supplied by the employer.

We need to have a balanced view of the relative power of workers in bureaucratic organizations. Workers' power position within specific organizations will depend, in part, on their capacity to reciprocate. In certain instances this capacity will be considerable. Organizational units that perform highly technical functions, such as planning and research, will be highly dependent on the expertise of organizational professionals. In addition, professionals will have substantial opportunities for career mobility, thus combining the capacity to reciprocate with the ability to seek benefits elsewhere. Peter Blau summarizes the argument and emphasizes that the capacity to provide unilateral services is a key condition of predominant power:

> Unilateral services that meet basic needs are the penultimate source of power. Its ultimate source, of course, is physical coercion. While the power that rests on coercion is more absolute ... it is also more limited in scope than the power that derives from met needs.[7]

POWER, VALUES, AND NEEDS

Key power decisions are made by those who are dominated as well as by those who dominate. The willingness of a subordinate to accept the benefits offered by a superior is a key condition of submission. Lack of power is rooted in the incapacity to reciprocate and in dependence on another's beneficence. It is vital, then, to examine the general origins of personal needs and how some may diverge from the "authentic" needs essential to personal development.

Development requires the satisfaction of material, security, affection, and esteem needs. These needs are rooted in "human nature" in the sense that all people have them from their earliest years. The particular quality of a need and its intensity will vary depending on the peculiarities of one's genetic inheritance and early social environment, but the presence of these needs is universal and undeniable.

It would be incorrect to argue that these basic needs are so clear that they automatically provide the criteria for deciding whether subordination is required in order to receive a benefit. The exchange of subordination for benefits will, in certain circumstances and for given individuals, constitute an explicit, conscious decision. More often, however, the decision to subordinate oneself is the product of acting on value premises that have been inculcated by dominant institutions such as the family, school, polity, and workplace. In some instances, what is valued may conflict with needs because values are largely the product of the social environment. We are not arguing here that individual needs and institutional values necessarily conflict, but only that they may. The following discussion illustrates this observation.

Some bureaucratic organizations require little innovation or technical skill for the effective performance of their functions. These organizations are most likely to be found where the technology of production is well developed and where the market or political environment is relatively stable. The primary organizational challenges under these conditions are to succeed in economizing rather than innovating. The emphasis on economizing requires the mastery of narrow, simple skills rather than the highly complex skills associated with innovation, change, and development.

The noninnovative organization can survive only if its employees do not expect the workplace to serve as an arena for satisfying development needs. Workers with such expectations in an economizing organization typically become very dissatisfied with the narrow, routinized technology. Such dissatisfaction may lead to strikes, demands for higher wages, changes in the technology, better fringe benefits, high rates of absenteeism, or high rates of turnover. Here we have an organizational dilemma: a mandatory, routinized technology on the one hand and worker dissatisfaction with it on the other. A logical alternative for the organization is to seek a change in the value premises that condition worker expectations and behavior.

Certain types of bureaucratic organizations encourage the expectation that work should satisfy primarily material interests and not personal development. Organizational denial of this need must be accompanied by an emphasis on the value of material benefits because the latter are more subject to manipulation and control by the organization. Inquiry into precisely how bureaucratic organizations attempt to control work values and the extent of that effort involves us in the root values inculcated by the school, family, and polity. The details of this subtle and complex process of diffusing bureaucratic values to these primary institutions is discussed in subsequent chapters.

POWER AND AUTHORITY

Widespread approval of a superior's domination transforms power into authority. Such authority is formed by mobilizing group authority and expectations behind the will of the superior, thus forcing individual conformity. What we see here is the emergence of a collective expectation or "rule" that the commands of the superior ought to be obeyed. In short, the transformation of power relationships into stabilized authority relationships requires the acceptance of the superior's power as legitimate and binding by a collectivity.

The significance of this transformation cannot be overstated. The authority of superiors is based on the feeling that subordination is a fair exchange for benefits received. When the power of the superior is transformed into authority, the relationship between the subordination required and the benefits received becomes less clear. In the extreme case, the benefit received by subordinates is the satisfaction of the value of subordination. Compliance with the commands of persons in positions of authority is the satisfaction that is used to justify subordination. From the organizational perspective this is a costless strategy of domination, but from the perspective of the individual it may mean the denial of needs.

INSTITUTIONAL POWER AND PERSONAL DEVELOPMENT

Within the broad categories of human needs there is also enormous individual variety. Development for the individual can take place only when a variety of value systems are permitted, thereby promoting various forms of need satisfaction. Further, the capacity to realize and sustain one's needs depends on developing strong attachments to a variety of institutions. It also depends on the capacity of these institutions to maintain the integrity of their core values. Affection, a need requisite to development, requires that family arrangements and the values they express permit the giving and receiving of love. The satisfaction of this need is not promoted when the bureaucratic value of impersonality pervades the value structure of the family so deeply that giving affection is regarded as undesirable or inconvenient. The diffusion of bureaucratic values to primary institutions can represent a major threat to personal development. The ability of institutions to maintain core values reflects their power relative to other institutions.

The capacity of institutions to retain some degree of autonomy depends on their being able to reciprocate the benefits received from other institutions. The autonomy of primary institutions from work organizations requires that they provide a "package" of benefits that work institutions value and that cannot be obtained elsewhere. If they are unable to reciprocate with valued benefits, and if they cannot repudiate the advantages of bureaucratic work institutions, they must offer their subordination in exchange for benefits.

Domination of one institution by another implies the capacity to influence institutional structure. We understand structure to mean the pattern of expectations for proper behavior; this may include skills as well as the type of feelings and the extent to which feelings should be displayed in connection with roles. These expectations reflect and express the more general values supported by the institution. Domination of one institution by another is the capacity to shape both institutional values and roles, and also the needs that can be satisfied by individuals in roles. For example, a major function of the polity is to set binding goals for the entire society. Democratic political systems emphasize the importance of widespread citizen participation in the problem-solving process as a core value. If a political system is dominated by bureaucratic work values that center around material advancement, and if participation can be shown to be unrelated to material advance, such participation is necessarily weakened. Political roles and processes valuing the participation of expert elites is the more likely result.

Institutional domination is the consequence of exchange. Although subordination is the price of being unable to reciprocate, it is not absolute. However weak the resource position of an institution, it usually is able to provide some benefit to dominant institutions. This suggests that the result of a power struggle is not necessarily the destruction but the incorporation of the weaker into the dominant institution. Incorporation is beneficial because it allows the exploitation of subordinate institutional resources and prevents the development of opposition. Incorporation is most effectively accomplished by exercising power "fairly." That is, the dominant institution makes it beneficial for the subordinate institution to continue its relationship.

SUMMARY OF ISSUES TO BE EXPLORED

Individual autonomy and balanced institutional power are preconditions of personal development. Individuals must have power within institutional settings, and primary institutions must be able to express their distinctive core values. Domination by a single institution or elite segment of it minimizes the likelihood of setting and attaining goals congruent with needs.

The diffusion of bureaucratic values to primary institutions and the individual consequences of this diffusion is the key issue we shall explore in this book. Pursuant to our understanding of power as exchange we shall (1) explore basic values expressed by the structure of bureaucratic institutions; (2) determine the extent to which these bureaucratic values have been diffused to or are shared by the school, family, and polity; and (3) assuming that bureaucratic values have in fact diffused to these institutions, examine the ways in which such diffusion has affected need satisfactions.

Chapter 2 explores the nature of bureaucracy and the values it expresses. This is followed by a discussion of needs Abraham Maslow says must be satisfied if self-actualization is to take place. In chapters 3 and 4 the diffusion of bureaucratic values to primary institutions is discussed. Chapter 3 focuses on microprocesses of socialization and reinforcement in the family, school, and polity. Chapter 4 links macroeconomic forces in industrial and postindustrial societies to the growth and diffusion of bureaucratic values. In chapter 5 the bureaucratically supportive and individually supportive ideal types are outlined for the family, polity, and school. Chapters 6, 7, and 8 deal with the empirical evidence on the extent to which families, schools, and polities approximate one or the other ideal type. The concluding chapter speculates about emerging changes in bureaucratic forms and their significance for personal development, trust and legitimacy in society.

2

Bureaucratic Values
and Personal Needs

As we have said, the power of bureaucracies derives from the acceptance of bureaucratic values. Conflict between bureaucratic values and individual needs has also been stressed. In this chapter we shall: (1) outline the major structural characteristics of bureaucracies and the values implied by them; (2) discuss self-actualization and other needs regarded by Maslow as fundamental; and (3) review how bureaucratic values interact with individual needs to produce what we shall call operational values. The discussion of values progresses in two parts. The first relates to values directly expressed by structural arrangements; the second deals with those that interact with individual needs.

BUREAUCRATIC STRUCTURE

The major ideas about the structure of bureaucracy stem from the classical theories of Max Weber.[1] Weber located the

roots of bureaucracy in the cultural traditions of Western society, particularly Western rationalism. Rationalism, according to
Weber, is a commitment that tends to pervade all aspects of
culture and takes many forms. Among the most important of
these are its manifestations in the economic system. The spirit
of rationalism in the economy is characterized by

> man (being) dominated by making money, where acquisition
> and action in pursuit of more acquisition become the ultimate
> purpose of life. Those in its spell cannot stand the waste of time
> in idle ramble or even in the spontaneous enjoyment of life. Life
> is to be spent in achieving. The pursuer of acquisition is restless-
> ly and constantly in action to achieve the maximum in the
> shortest time possible. He advocates greater efficiency, since
> this leads to more results in his incessant fervent striving. He
> acts systematically, generating and building systems of action in
> calculation and anticipation of others' actions. He is under con-
> stant urge to rationalize his enterprise.... Credibility, punc-
> tuality, honesty, inventiveness, adaptability to new circum-
> stances are prized by him, since such qualities are instrumental
> in efforts to achieving.... He... has little regard for traditions,
> which often look to him as fetters impeding his climb to wealth,
> and from there to still greater wealth.[2]

The cultural commitment to rationalism has several value components. According to this tradition, one's life is not centered
around the attainment of substantive goals or the spontaneous
enjoyment of events, but around processes for achieving goals.
For example, time should be used economically and efficiently.
One should constantly strive to improve one's capacity for engaging in goal-attaining processes. Self-improvement is defined
largely in terms of improving one's calculative ability; acting
"rationally" means acting impersonally. Tradition, personal attachment, and sentiment are rejected as bases for action because
they reduce the instrumental quality of decisions. As circumstances change, one must inventively adapt to new condi-

tions. What matters is dynamic instrumental activity as such, not the goals that such activity theoretically serves.

Kenneth McNeil notes that "Weber did not insist that consequences had to be rational, only that the consequences had to be traced back causally to modes of calculation in the heads of managerial elites."[3] This is illustrated by the emphasis on rules. Weber thought that rules enhance the instrumental quality of organizations not because they always lead to more effective or more efficient decisions but because they provide a "public" basis for organizational decisions. Ideally, rules are known to all and are applied in an impartial fashion. Not all problems faced by bureaucratic organizations can be anticipated in the form of rules, however.

Much of bureaucratic life involves responding to unanticipated changes. This means that more general mechanisms of instrumental rationality must be included in the bureaucratic model. Two of the more important of these mechanisms are specialization and hierarchical authority. The discretionary right to decide, according to Weber, is vested in positions with fixed and limited authority. Associated with a particular position are rights to make identified types of decisions. Limits on authority to decide serves two instrumental purposes. First, it helps ensure the expertise of the decision-maker. Second, it makes the decision "traceable" in the sense of accountability and responsibility for it.

According to the model, bureaucratic positions are ordered along horizontal and vertical dimensions. Vertical ordering implies a positional hierarchy of authority in which those in superior positions have the right to supervise the work of those in subordinate positions. In the "monocratic" form of bureaucracy, the positional hierarchy is organized so that each subordinate has but one superior. The monocratic hierarchy was regarded by Weber as rational because it serves to coordinate discretionary decisions. Positional specialization is important because it enhances expertise, but it creates problems of coordination between specialists. The basic justification for hierarchy then is to coordinate among these specialized discretionary decisions.

The values expressed by bureaucratic structures — namely, impersonal relations, hierarchy, and specialization — are reinforced by the career pattern of the bureaucratic official. Specialization and expertise are developed through training before joining the organization as well as through in-service training. Beyond these formal prerequisites for holding a bureaucratic role, there are certain emotional prerequisites. We have noted that impersonality is central. This means that in the development of a career, the bureaucrat must demonstrate enthusiasm for work, but at the same time this must not extend to the point of mixing private feelings, emotions, or interests with the conduct of organizational business. Private and official activity are separated in a number of ways, including rules against nepotism, against engaging in outside activity that involves a conflict of interest with organizational activity, against using organizational property and equipment for personal purposes, and so on.

The bureaucratic model offers a substantive theory of exchange between the bureaucrat and the organization. Specialization, expertise, impersonality, and hierarchy are the central elements of instrumental rationality that bureaucratic officials contribute to the organization. The officials, in turn, are attracted to the organization and motivated to contribute by inducements of material advancement, security, and career mobility.

From the perspective of the bureaucracy, it is important that there be a large pool of workers who value instrumental rationality and who are attracted by the inducements of advancement, security, and career mobility. The power of bureaucracies is dependent on sustaining these values, an argument elaborated in chapter 1. Given these bureaucratic values, the next issue involves an examination of the needs that must be satisfied for personal development. What are these needs and to what extent are they congruent with bureaucratic values?

SELF-ACTUALIZATION AND HUMAN NEEDS

The idea of personal development figures prominently in the writings of Abraham Maslow.[4] The core of Maslow's theory of human development involves identification of five basic needs. These needs are physiological, safety or security, affection and belonging, esteem, and self-actualization. The first four needs differ in that they are preconditions for the fifth need. Needs constitute a hierarchy or scale. The needs at the bottom of the hierarchy must be met before those at the higher levels can be satisfied. Thus, if one's need for safety is not satisfied, it will be impossible to self-actualize. Similarly, one who has not received adequate affection as a child will be unable to satisfy self-actualization needs.

The most primitive needs identified by Maslow are physiological—the needs of food, sex, shelter, clothing, and the like. Knutson has pointed out that "persons who have never had their physiological needs fulfilled will not be open to the concerns of those people who have—no matter what their current social status."[5] This view underscores the centrality of early years in the individual's development; that is, even if early deprivation is overcome in later years, one will continue to react to the environment as if one were materially deprived. It is likely that such a person will be fearful of and passive toward the environment, conservative in attitude, and self-oriented. The individual who has met these needs in childhood, on the other hand, may move on to seek fulfillment of security needs.

The needs of security, affection, and belonging relate to an emotional atmosphere that is loving, predictable, and stable. Insecurity may be rooted in physical displacement, such as forced family separation due to war or work. It may also be rooted in the instability of parent-child relations. Borel has summarized this situation in the following way:

> If the parents are themselves...unable to follow a constant and predictable pattern of response, the child is faced with the impossible situation of trying to find security in a desperate struggle where the rules are...changing. He repeatedly tries to solve the dilemma by alternatives of independent action and is just as constantly thwarted until he finally gives up. He becomes conditioned to the attitude that what little security is available lies in dependence on others and the anxiety-ridden struggle to gain the approval and good will of others is the only way of life. He then spends his life acting out roles that he feels will gratify others while carrying a...burden of anger and frustration.[6]

The need for affection and belonging is similar to that of security, but differs from the latter because it implies greater mutuality between persons and does not emphasize stability. The family looms large because love and affection in the early years can only be supplied through persistent, face-to-face contact. Where this love has not been forthcoming and where attempts at loving have not been accepted, the child is likely to express hostility and aggression toward others. Berelson and Steiner indicate that "in general, the unloved child tends to be an unloving adult, with a high degree of self-hatred (that is, unlovable)." The consequence is an outward glorification of authority figures because of the importance of love for the individual but, at the same time, deep hostility toward those figures perceived as unfairly withholding needed affection.

The need for affection and belonging is to be distinguished from the need for esteem primarily in terms of the basis for acceptance by others.[7] In the case of esteem, acceptance reflects an attribution of competence and prestige. The basis of recognition is not a general emotional commitment.

In studies that have concerned themselves with the problem of esteem development, the family again is central. Coopersmith states:

> The mothers of children with low self-esteem are less affectionate and accepting and ... their children perceive them in just this way.... The whole tenor of the results so far supports the general hypothesis that parental rejection results in feelings of personal insignificance.[8]

While the family is the major source of personal esteem, the attribution of prestige, competence, and status can be accomplished by more impersonal secondary institutions such as the school or place of work. Elaborate mechanisms are available in both settings to provide prestige to those who conform to institutional expectations.

According to Maslow, adult behavior that is motivated by the desire to fulfill unmet physiological, security, and esteem needs is termed "deficiency motivated." Such individuals tend to share the view that human beings are weak and untrustworthy, that human needs are insatiable, and that one's environment is insecure, hostile, and unmanageable. As Knutson has noted, such a view leads to a posture of defensiveness, generally equates inaction with security, and makes any action seem extreme because the threat is perceived as extreme. Deficiency-motivated behaviors are characterized by a tendency to be unrealistic in one's perception of the environment, to be fearful of what the future holds, and to be hostile to the world that seems so threatening.

The self-actualizing individual is held to be highly aware of self and others, universalistic in thoughts and values rather than personalistic, and a creative and inquiring person. The preconditions for self-actualization include satisfaction of deprivation needs. Self-actualization depends on the individual "being motivated by some values which he strives for or gropes for and to which he is loyal." Among the most important of these are democratic values. "Responsibility for oneself and others, especially in the democratic use of power over other people, demands education and knowledge, as autocratic submission... does not."[9]

The development of the self-actualizing individual depends not only on the quality of interpersonal relations in the family and school but also on positive incentives provided by the political culture. The individual must have opportunities for participating in important decisions and must value those opportunities. Those who are potential self-actualizers and who find themselves in an authoritarian, nonparticipatory political culture may become alienated, tension ridden, and hostile because they see the opportunity and importance of self-actualization while being denied it.

OPERATIONAL VALUES

The characteristics of bureaucracy that were noted above and attributed to Max Weber represent objective characteristics of bureaucratic organizations. Here we are concerned with the personal values that are created when human beings interact with these bureaucratic aspects of their environment. Bureaucratic workplaces shape the values of workers. "Operational values" describes those values that are created in the workplace to satisfy bureaucratic ends but that may be inconsistent with personal needs and development.[10] We address operational values here because they may ultimately be diffused to the family, school, and polity.

Victor Thompson[11] has given special attention to the personal consequences of bureaucratic characteristics. Bureaucracies are powerful in part because they provide job security and material advancement. Thompson argues that the satisfaction of security and material needs results in a work environment characterized by anxiety, tension, and alienation rather than a sense of fulfillment and personal development. To understand these consequences, it is necessary to recall and reappraise two root characteristics of bureaucratic structure: specialization and hierarchy.

Specialization is of two major types. The first deals with the nature of tasks, the second with the adaptation of the individual to particular circumstances. The second type, specialization of person, implies that the individual has developed a complex set of skills, behavioral responses, and qualities that promise better adaptation to particular circumstances. Specialization of task implies movement in the opposite direction. Instead of more complexity of skills and patterns of behavior, the movement is toward repetitive routines and a narrower set of skills. The stereotype of this kind of specialization is found on the assembly line. The worker may become more skilled in the performance of tasks over time, but the range of skills is not expanded.

Specialization as personal adaptation suggests that the individual is less dependent on the environment. It differs from task specialization in that it depends more on the skills the worker possesses than on those possessed by others. The person specialized in the sense of adaptation is hence a powerful person because she or he is not as compelled as others to engage in subordination to satisfy basic needs.

Specialization in bureaucracies, at least at the lower levels, is of the task type. The life blood of bureaucratic systems is the capacity to divide required tasks into narrow, homogeneous units. Homogeneity of skill reduces the time it takes to master the task and minimizes any disruption caused when a worker leaves a position. Greater task specialization increases one's dependence on fellow workers and on the organization, but reduces the centrality of any one worker.

Specialization of person does not imply that interdependence in organizations is unnecessary. Organizational missions are complex. The central issue from this perspective is the kind and conditions of interdependence. Specialization of person allows the worker to perform a significant social function and allows the exercise and development of personal skills. The interdependence of those with complex skills comes from a mutual recognition that support is necessary to perform one's function. This is to be contrasted with the situation in which interdependence is enforced through a narrowing of skills and through insistence on a steeply graded structure of formal authority.

Hierarchy is a system of superior-subordinate roles. A role is a set of mutual expectations held of persons in positions, including expectations for behavior and the rewards associated with that behavior. Blau notes that these expectations have two distinct elements.

> The expectation that the other's conduct conform to accepted social standards, otherwise he would not make an enjoyable companion, and the expectation that associating with him would furnish particular rewards, more or less than associating with someone else.[12]

These expectations are hierarchical insofar as they result in the mutual expectation of subordination of one to another. Subordination, as we learned from the earlier discussion of exchange, is the result of the perception that one is receiving benefits that are regarded as essential, that cannot be obtained elsewhere, and that cannot be matched by providing equally attractive benefits.

The subordination of roles that results from exchange processes in organizations is different from what Weber refers to in his discussion of bureaucracy. For Weber, subordination is based on the hierarchy of formal authority, that is, authority based on some type of legislative or legal statement. From the perspective of social exchange, subordination results from the allocation of benefits.

Formal superiors are often in a position to provide material benefits such as salary increases, promotion, and tenure. Beyond meeting these material needs, superiors are able to affect conditions relating to esteem and personal development. Evaluation is important for salary, but it is also important for prestige and social status attributed by coworkers. Positive evaluations are likely to enhance one's position in status and prestige systems and enhance one's sense of self-esteem. The attribution of prestige and status may also increase the capacity to achieve personal development through greater power and autonomy. High status and prestige may enable subordinates to achieve a relatively more independent power position in the organization. For example, favorable evaluation is likely to result in increasing the worth of one's advice which will, through exchange processes, enhance power. Independent power allows one to establish goals consistent with personal needs. Independent power also means a greater likelihood of having the material and human means necessary to achieve these goals.

The consequences of bureaucratic structure for operational values depend on such factors as personality, social class origins, and alternatives to bureaucratic employment. Robert Presthus suggests that the majority of people in bureaucratic organizations may be described as actual or potential "indifferents." That is, they have opted out of the struggle for bureaucratic rewards in part because of a realistic assessment that they will not be successful. They have come to terms with their work environment through psychological withdrawal and the redirection of interests toward nonwork satisfactions.[13] Our major focus is not on indifferents but on those who have either attained or hope to attain relatively high organizational positions. Those occupying subordinate roles are not as important for understanding bureaucratic power because they have little control over values that are diffused to the family, school, and polity. These values are largely under the control of institutional elites.[14]

Victor Thompson argues that the task requirements of high-level positions tend to be vague and the criteria of adequate performance difficult to articulate and measure.[15] This vagueness is particularly characteristic of governmental organizations where goals often are unclearly stated and where goal accomplishment is difficult if not impossible to measure. This vagueness results in anxiety and tension if the official is

committed to career mobility, material advancement, and job
security. Without relatively objective criteria for effective performance, the upwardly mobile person is faced with constant
career uncertainty. The official may adapt to this uncertainty in
the following ways:

> Since the distribution of...[bureaucratic rewards] is the
> prerogative of a superior, the satisfaction of goals requires con-
> formity to the superior's demands, whatever they may be. Thus
> "brown-nosing," hypocrisy, and "false personalization" are
> endemic in modern bureaucracies. This is especially true in the
> higher reaches of the hierarchy. Anxiety generated by non-
> operational demands of superiors and by the actual dependence
> on subordinates often expresses itself in a preference for
> bureaupathic practices, such as excessive formalism and imper-
> sonality, overstrict compliance, rules and regulations and close
> supervision.[16]

The official usually adapts to the ambiguity of performance expectations by developing a pleasant, cordial, supportive stance
towards superiors. But the anxiety rooted in the fundamental
diffuseness of one's career requires release and is often expressed in demands for control over the behavior of subordinates, enforced by an elaborate set of rules and regulations
and by an insistence on the rights and prerogatives of one's position. The demand for control over subordinates serves the dual
functions of allowing the release of tension that develops from
career uncertainty and of assuring that subordinates do not
engage in behaviors that will displease those who control access
to higher organizational positions.

    In addition to satisfying the demand for control and false
personalism, impersonality is also characteristic of the upwardly mobile's operational value orientation. Impersonality here is
not used in the same sense as Weber. Weber was concerned that
organizational effectiveness would be diminished if decisions
were made according to criteria of personal rather than organizational benefit. The impersonality that is the consequence of

hierarchy reflects the fear of being influenced and controlled by (rather than controlling) subordinates. Impersonality towards subordinates is protective of the superior because it allows treatment of subordinates as objects that must be controlled to achieve organizational purposes. The justification of subordinate control is weakened where they are regarded as capable and competent and where they are treated as individuals having needs beyond economic reward.

The original Weberian model of bureaucracy sought to combine hierarchical power and expertise of specialization while assigning interpersonal sentiments and feelings to neutral ground. The reconciliation of expertise and power was based on the assumption that organizational mobility and increases in hierarchical power would be based on objective merit. Thompson and Presthus, by contrast, indicate how sentiments seriously transform the practical meaning of the bureaucratic model.

The often obscure technical nature of merit together with the power orientation of "upward mobiles" has the effect of making values of power, subordination, and hierarchy dominant, while technical expertise remains subordinate. Indeed, one can argue that interpersonal skill and false personalism are more important operational values than expertise, once the priority of power is recognized. This inversion of the relative importance of power, impersonality, and expertise is of enormous importance for primary institutions and the support they provide for personal development.

The importance of bureaucratic values is not limited to their direct effects on organizational participants. As we have suggested earlier, it is important to explore how and to what extent these values have been diffused to the family, school, and polity. The basic question is: How do primary institutions meet needs if there has been diffusion to them of the bureaucratic values we have described?

As was suggested in the discussion of social exchange, the power of bureaucratic organizations is substantially enhanced if its values are inculcated by primary institutions. In chapter 3 we explore the socialization of individuals to bureaucratic values by primary institutions. In chapter 4 we show how primary institutions themselves have been shaped to serve as agents of socialization by industrial forces.

3

The Diffusion
of Bureaucratic Values

THE OPERATIONAL VALUES of bureaucracies are primary vehicles for bureaucratic power. The consequences of bureaucratic power for need satisfaction and personal development must be examined in the context of primary institutions such as the family, school, and polity. These institutions are inseparable from the process of personal development. The central problem here is to examine the processes through which bureaucratic values are diffused to individuals. How could families, schools, and political communities have come to "internalize" and transmit bureaucratic values and in that process seriously reduce their capacity to fulfill certain traditional, nonbureaucratic, and unique functions essential for the growth of the individual?

SOCIALIZATION AS DIFFUSION

Values, including bureaucratic ones, are often learned through socialization.[1] Socialization is an educational or

29

inculcative process through which one internalizes values and attitudes found in the social environment. The social environment is an enormously complicated system of cues, demands, norms, standards, information, and values to which each individual is related. The values to which one is socialized are potentially diverse and sometimes contradictory. In the family setting a child may be taught the virtue of loyalty to parents, even at the price of telling outsiders untruths; in the school setting the same child may learn the moral and practical virtues of telling the truth even at the risk of disloyalty to family members.

Within the social environment there are agents of socialization, specific persons or groups, whose values are transmitted and adopted. A basic question about socialization is how the process of transmission from agents takes place. This question will be examined in the specific institutional contexts of the family, school, and polity. As we have noted, these institutions serve as vehicles for diffusing bureaucratic values. But it is equally true that they themselves are shaped by other outside pressures. The discussion of the latter issue is reserved for the next chapter, which is an historical sketch of these outside pressures and influences. Here we shall outline two major types of socialization and how they are expressed by the primary institutions.

MODELING AND INSTRUMENTAL TRAINING

Individuals are socialized in two ways. The first is through instrumental training by agents with specific goals (cooperation, efficiency, productivity, to name a few) in mind. Instrumental training is someone's conscious strategy of rewarding persons for engaging in approved behavior that is necessary (instrumental) in attaining some further end. A good example is encouraging school children to help formulate rules of classroom conduct. Such participation tends to produce a sense of influence or mastery over the environment. This in turn contributes to a feeling that obeying rules is pretty much like obeying one's own "true" wishes. Positive reinforcement through participatory rewards may fail, however. A strategy of negative reinforcement (punishment) may then be utilized, such as denying children classroom or school yard privileges.

The second type of socialization, modeling, is a process in which the explicit inculcation of values is rejected in favor of presenting the young with attractive role models whose values and behavior are emulated. Underlying this approach is the theory that individuals tend to imitate the behavior of "significant others" if imitation results in rewards.

The behavior of role models is often complicated and surrounded by circumstances imperfectly understood by the erstwhile imitator. How individuals link reward expectations to their own behavior is not very clearly understood, but it does appear to involve several known mechanisms. One of these is that emulation of a model is a trial-and-error process; the model is the source of rewards, the conferral of which tends to "reinforce" behavior similar to that of the model. Failure to repeat role model behavior carries no reward and hence may result in feelings of deprivation or anxiety. The antidote, of course, is to return to behavior that emulates the model and therefore is rewarded. At an early age the child tends to obey parents partly to satisfy needs — food, love, security, and so on. In this case we may say that obedient behavior is the result of reinforcement by the parental model. In time, however, obedience may become detached from practical incentives such as love and security; obedience results simply because it is, in itself, satisfying and because anxiety is caused by nonobedient behavior. Thus what begins as a trial-and-error search for need satisfaction ends as routinized behavior enforced by the desire to avoid anxiety.

Some of the major points about role models in the specific context of family socialization are well made in the following legend:

A townsman had requested that the Rabbi pray to insure that his son would study the Torah diligently. In reply to this man's request, the Rabbi said: "If your sons will see that you are a diligent student, they will imitate you. But if you neglect your own studies, and merely wish your sons to study, the result will be that they will do likewise when they grow up; they will neglect the Torah themselves and desire that their sons do the studying."[2]

The legend suggests, of course, that children are more apt to be impressed with and follow what their parents do than what they say. The importance of this observation for the present analysis can be put as follows: through their function as role models for children, parents can become diffusers of bureaucratic values. The behavior, and the values implied by it, become especially pertinent to the bureaucratic diffusion process when it is generalized to other situations. Imitative behavior in one area may be extended to a variety of others. An example is the value of tidy housekeeping. "A mother's behavior may exemplify that value," says Gewirtz, "and her daughter either may be directly reinforced for...tidying...or may exhibit those responses through simple generalized imitation [of the mother's behavior]."[3]

Modeling and reinforcement as mechanisms of bureaucratic diffusion imply that the individual's mind is a *tabula rasa* on which a tremendous variety of environmental influences are imprinted. According to this view, the mind reacts rather than acts, suggesting that values are implanted and absorbed rather than deliberately or consciously chosen. But this view must not be carried too far. Certain cognitive standards are employed by the individual to decide whether particular values will be accepted. New values may be rejected because they conflict with old ones. Or values may come into conflict, as when the value of self-sacrifice learned in the family collides with that of success and achievement in the classroom. Because value conflicts occur, we may regard the socialization process as one in which the child absorbs information, norms, and values that may become dissonant or incompatible. These value conflicts are important for the success of bureaucratic diffusion, organizational control over workers, and personal development.

It was suggested in chapter 2 that organizational control of subordinate values is a relatively costless strategy of domination, and that the substitution of organizational values for individual needs may result in the frustration of personal development. Personal development is more likely to take place when a variety of value systems are permitted and when a variety of need satisfaction forms are permitted.

The presence of conflicting patterns of socialization and differing values in the socialization process are evidence that there has been exposure to alternative models of personal realization. To the extent that the diffusion process and its agents are "captured" by a single set of values, the possibilities of personal development are correspondingly narrowed. It is important then to understand if the primary socialization institutions are captured in a similar way or whether they remain inculcators of significantly different values.

SCHOOLS AS MODELS OF WORK PLACES

That schools are an important link in the formation of values is hardly subject to debate. Public law typically requires school attendance until the age of sixteen. In 1970, 91 percent of all white and 86 percent of all black Americans between the ages of sixteen and seventeen were enrolled in school.[4] What is important in the educational experience is not just the great amount of time spent in school but also the intensity and pervasiveness of student exposure to values.

Schooling entails complex activities and attachments with peers, teachers, counselors, academic programs, and social programs. It also involves such routines as recitation in class, recess, lunch, and assemblies. All of these activities, attachments, and routines shape the child's sense of what the world is like and should be like. The school is typically the first occasion where a child is exposed to behavioral norms in an organizational setting. The child also learns that behavioral conformity serves values whose validity is not easily challenged.

Michael Katz[5] argues that the organizational structure of the public schools in the United States since the 1880s has remained the same—bureaucratic—and that they were so structured because of the perceived need to inculcate students with certain values and attitudes. "The purpose of the school system and its structure are clearly interrelated," says Katz. School officials "understood that part of the message they wished to have transmitted, the attitudes they wished formed, would inhere in the structural arrangements themselves rather than in explicit didactic procedures."[6] School structure constitutes in itself a normative model of significant importance for value socialization.

There are several different types of school structure. Grannis suggests an important distinction between factory and corporation schools. The factory school originated in the late nineteenth century in urban areas. Its primary purpose was to inculcate in the lower class, including immigrants, values consistent with increasing the industrial output of standardized products. The corporation school, a spin-off from the factory school and one that is increasing in importance, was designed to meet the needs of large bureaucracies, especially those of problem solving and innovation. The values served and diffused by these different types of schools are not difficult to differentiate.

The essence of the factory-type school is found in the bureaucratic values of specialization, hierarchy, and instrumentalism. Specialization is modeled to students by teachers whose comparatively narrow fields of expertise lead to their recognition as classroom specialists. They diffuse the value of specialization by assigning identical standards and requiring standardized classroom recitation by each student.[7] Specialization is also modeled by tracking students into vocational or collegiate programs. Hierarchy is modeled by a teacher who is "in charge" and has the power and authority to confer positive or negative sanctions. "Normal" grading curves that differentiate high from low performers serve a similar function.

Instrumentalism is expressly inculcated in the later school years when students, presumably having internalized the proper values, are encouraged to pursue learning that is "practical" so that they will "find a place in life," "earn a living," or "enjoy the good things of life." The student is encouraged to see the difference between education that is "liberalizing" or "abstract," and that which serves as an instrument for the attainment of practical goals.

One of the major differences between the factory and corporation school is the latter's emphasis on interpersonal relations. The corporation school includes team-teaching. Team-teaching recognizes the different capacities of teachers. However, specialized competence is exercised in a collective setting. The planning, teaching, and evaluation of instruction is done as a group. The presumed advantage of this group approach is that it forces teachers to explain their techniques to peers and receive constructive comments. Unlike the factory school, there is not an assumption of "the one best way." Rather, complexity and change are coped with through group problemsolving. Interpersonal skill is both learned and essential for group-centered learning.

In ideal terms the corporation school is designed to recognize the unique capacities and stages of development of each student. This is done through techniques for individual student evaluation and through individualized instruction.

> Students and teachers are grouped in numerous ways for various purposes, and complex schedules evolve to allocate the time and resources of the school.... It is not mere availability of these resources that leads to their use in the corporation school.

The whole attitude of the school is oriented toward planning and rationalization and toward the employment of specialized skills and technology.[8]

The corporation school might be regarded as a sophisticated system for inculcating specialized skills, but beyond this the evidence is that it tends to breed a deep sense of subordination and false personalism. The fact that teachers plan and evaluate collectively makes it very difficult to adapt spontaneously to situational needs. Collective decision-making and attendant collective responsibility for the curriculum make the teacher reluctant to engage in spot changes. Because the scheduling and programming of instruction is so complex, spontaneous changes imply considerable instructional disruption for other students and teachers. The factory school tends to develop relatively close and stable personal relationships. In the corporation school, social relationships with both students and teachers are much less stable and enduring. The mode of instruction moves the student through a relatively larger number of social relationships. Furthermore, "the teachers consciously construe their role as more professional and less nurturing."[9]

Students in the corporation school acquire skills essential to the smooth functioning of large bureaucratic organizations. The corporation school provides a model of society that is complexly organized, where highly specialized skills are prized and where smooth yet impersonal relations are valued. Significantly, corporation schools tend to be found in middle-class communities and school districts where parents are likely to hold middle-level positions in bureaucratic organizations. Corporation schools appear to inculcate precisely those values and skills necessary to function effectively in middle-level bureaucratic positions.

The contrasts between factory and corporation schools suggest that the diffusion process is not a single one through which a uniform set of bureaucratic values is transmitted. Bureaucratic organizations require a variety of skills and commitments; diffusing institutions reflect these varying needs. In the following section the idea of variation in values diffused is elaborated. We shall show how variations in work conditions affect the diffusion process taking place in the family.

VARIATIONS IN FAMILY SOCIALIZATION TO BUREAUCRATIC VALUES

Variations in work values transmitted to children may reflect differences in feelings of autonomy and power in their parents' work environment. This means that the greater the parents' control of their material resources and activities, the greater the likelihood that autonomy will be reflected in the values to which the children are exposed in the family setting. A father with little work autonomy, habituated to following "detailed specifications of how he will use...time,...energy, and...interest" is apt to create the same experiences at home for his children.[10] A father experiencing deprivation and frustration at his workplace is apt to fashion a home environment that does the same for his children. Generalizing somewhat, it can be said that the degree of subordination demands on children is often a function of greater or lesser autonomy at the workplace. Parents having much autonomy at work will place a lower emphasis on obedience than those who experience little or no autonomy. Autonomous parents are less inclined to resort to severe techniques of discipline, such as corporal punishment, and more inclined to depend on reason or the use of guilt as control devices.

Miller and Swanson[11] look at the impact of work on value diffusion from a different angle. They distinguish between entrepreneurial and bureaucratic family types. This distinction is useful because it illustrates possible variations in socialization associated with different work environments. In the entrepreneurial family, the parent is responsible for running a business or works in a small firm. The bureaucratic family is one in which the parent works in a large organization. Rather than dealing with levels of autonomy, the authors seek to explain child-rearing patterns as reflections of the values that insure success in these different work settings.

The values for entrepreneurial parents are self-control and self-denial, and the capacity to use one's time, energy, and resources in the most judicious and effective manner. The father is "ever conscious of his future, husbanding his time and contacts and savings and skills for use at the most propitious moment." His behavior is like his money: it must be carefully invested. "Such conditions put a premium on controlled, rational behavior, on ignoring the impulse of the moment in the interest of long-range prospects."[12] The child brought up under these conditions is quickly taught that success depends on personal effort and that the work area is one in which resourceful and skillful persons can capitalize on the many opportunities available. As should be apparent, some aggressive behavior is encouraged in achieving one's personal goals.

Entrepreneurial values such as self-denial and independence are transmitted through parentally imposed reinforcements. Self-indulgent behaviors such as thumbsucking and masturbation are prohibited; conscious attempts are made to break ties with other family members through exposure to other persons. Children are denied assistance in problem solving until it is clear that solutions are beyond the child's capabilities.

Much of the foregoing stands in vivid contrast to patterns of child rearing in bureaucratic families. While socialization in such families also draws heavily on conditions at the workplace (particularly such bureaucratic factors as complexity, interpersonal communications, and hierarchy), "bureaucratic" children are less self-controlled and more skilled at interpersonal relations. At the higher reaches of bureaucratic organizations where size and complexity create serious problems of communications, the ability to resolve such problems through smooth interpersonal relations is rewarded. Such capacity is carried home as well and becomes part of the socialization of children.

Hierarchy implies the acceptance of superiors. Unlike the entrepreneurial setting, where independent thought and behavior are encouraged, the bureaucratic setting strongly emphasizes deference to those in superior positions. Carried to the context of child rearing, deference for the child means that superiors must be regarded not as hateful figures to be challenged but rather as skillful and sensitive individuals deserving of emulation and cooperation.[13] Thumbsucking is thus viewed positively because it teaches a method of relaxing that does not make demands on others. Prolonged nursing and feeding "on demand" are used to encourage a benign view of parents as authorities.

The distinction between entrepreneurial and bureaucratic family types is diminishing in relevance since opportunities for entrepreneurial work are declining rapidly. This implies a growth in bureaucratic-type families. It is important to ask if differences within bureaucratic structures (in the sense of differences in role, function, or status) lead to differences in patterns of child rearing and value inculcation. For example, what is the evidence that those who have exhibited successful upward mobility in a bureaucratic setting tend to prize autonomy, self-direction, and personal achievement more than those at lower rungs on the bureaucratic ladder? The question is important because we want to know whether the apparent variations in values diffused to children can be explained by variations in bureaucratic positions.

Unfortunately, students of bureaucracy have not systematically explored the impact of bureaucratic position on values and socialization. Little is known about the relationship between parental work position and socialization to values in the family setting. One aspect of this problem has been discussed by Melvin Kohn, who sought to determine the extent to which parents in high bureaucratic positions value self-direction and consciously seek to transmit that value to their children.

Kohn defines self-direction as "the use of initiative, thought, and independent judgment in work." He suggests two general conditions of self-direction closely approximating the facts of work-life found at upper bureaucratic levels: (1) Self-direction implies the relative absence of close supervision. Constant monitoring of work is lacking but there is a presumption that work is performed according to well-defined and well-understood standards. (2) More importantly,

> the work, in its very substance, requires initiative, thought, and independent judgment. Work with data or with people is more likely to require initial thought and judgment than is work with things. Complex work with data or with people—synthesizing or coordinating data, teaching or negotiating with people—is especially likely to require initiative, thought, and judgment.[14]

Kohn's research tends to confirm the idea that opportunity for self-direction in work is positively associated with attempts to inculcate the value of self-direction in children. The type and intensity of self-direction found at various levels of bureaucracy was found to be closely correlated with the type and intensity of self-direction transmitted by parents to their children. Miller and Swanson believe that such similarity in the two institutions (bureaucracy and family) implies a social logic in which children are exposed to values in the family that will prepare them as adults for the work environment they will occupy in future years.

The school and the family, we have noted, are powerful socializing agents and therefore central to the understanding of bureaucratic diffusion. We would be remiss, however, not to note the role of political institutions and the political system in the diffusion process.

THE ROLE OF POLITICAL INSTITUTIONS IN DIFFUSION

A major function of the polity is to establish public policies that are binding on citizens. The most direct expression of public policy is legislative statute. But more important for the process of value diffusion are the ways in which statutes are implemented by governmental bureaucracies. One of the most dramatic examples of this is found in the area of governmental welfare policy.

Piven and Cloward[15] note that governmental welfare bureaucracies have been particularly successful in reinforcing the value placed on hard work, achievement, and expertise by both the poor and the middle class. The learning of these values is induced, particularly in the case of the poor, through the extensive use of negative sanctions, including the degradation of welfare recipients. "A central feature of the recipient's degradation is that she must surrender commonly accepted rights in exchange for aid."[16] Mothers of dependent children are often asked to answer questions about their sexual behavior and have their homes subject to searches and surveillance. In addition, it is common for the mass media to dramatize legislative investigations and exposes of alleged "sexual immorality," "chiseling," and "malingering" among welfare recipients.

Piven and Cloward note that welfare recipients not only submit to these attacks but even endorse the value premises upon which they are based. For example,

> even on those rare occasions when groups of recipients do rise up to protest their treatment by relief agencies — such as the demonstrations recently organized by the National Welfare Rights Organization — work thus is reaffirmed even as relief restrictions are condemned. Some AFDC mothers *with four or five young children* [emphasis supplied] who picket welfare departments for more money now! also carry signs proclaiming we want jobs![17]

Piven and Cloward conclude by noting that because work values are so powerful, welfare recipients are willing to accept almost any type of work, whatever the wage or the child-rearing obligations of the mothers.

The transmission of bureaucratic values through public policy must be understood in part as a consequence of the needs of political institutions. That is, while public policy may express political interests outside formal political institutions such as the Congress, presidency, or courts, it is also the product of the internal needs of political institutions. This is quite clear in the case of public bureaucracies.

Anthony Downs[18] asks: Why do bureaucracies develop ideologies? An ideology, as Downs defines it, has a major component of value. An ideology is "a verbal image of that part of the good society relevant to the functions of the particular bureaucracy concerned, plus the chief means of constructing that portion."[19] Such ideologies are important for diffusion because they shape the details of day-to-day administration and the ways in which bureaucrats interact with clients. Bureaucratic ideologies, according to Downs, are developed because they are efficient means of communicating with certain groups both inside and outside bureaus. Each bureau exists only as long as it continues to persuade external groups with control over resources that it deserves continued support. Because those who need to be persuaded of the value of a bureaucracy's operation seldom have the time and energy to learn the details of its operations, administrative advocates resort to generalized bureaucratic images or ideologies. The ideologies are effective in bringing support to the organization insofar as they convincingly show a linkage between bureaucratic policy and the interests of key public and private elites.

Bureaucratic ideologies and the specific values comprising them not only help mobilize external support but also facilitate the coordination of internal bureaucratic operations. Bureaucracies tend to be large. Positions are occupied by a vast array of persons with different technical specialties. Hence there needs to be some mechanism to convey the overriding purpose of organizational action. Size and specialization imply a threat to the coordinated execution of organizational missions. One way to deal with this threat is to institutionalize premises that provide a common direction for organizational decisions.

The importance of organizational ideologies for maintenance of organizational support is reflected in their content. First, they usually emphasize the benefits rather than the costs of administrative programs. Second, they often imply a developmental dynamic in which the functions of the organization must be expanded rather than contracted or maintained. Third, the organizational ideology will usually stress the high level of coordination and efficiency of operations.

For example, the Tennessee Valley Authority is an independent government corporation with extensive multifunctional responsibilities in the areas of agriculture, conservation, and electrical energy development. In terms of functional scope and independence of operation, its organization was unprecedented for a governmental entity. The "grass roots" ideology of the Tennessee Valley Authority was essential, particularly in its early years, because the TVA could not take its continued existence for granted. From the very beginning, severe attacks, particularly by private producers of electrical power, were common. For many, it was regarded as the first major expression of American state socialism. The major response to these external threats was to develop the grass roots ideology, which had a substantial effect not only on TVA operations and goals but also on the patterns of interaction between TVA and its various clients in the Tennessee Valley.

The essentials of the grass roots ideology were, first, that the responsible agency in the area of operation is permitted the freedom to make significant decisions on its own account. Stated negatively, the responsible agency should not be made a part of a larger centralized administrative unit based in Washington, D.C. Second, there must be active participation by the people in the areas affected by the programs of the enterprise. The services of state and local agencies were to be utilized with the objective of strengthening their role in the life of the local citizenry, but with federal leadership. Third, the decentralized administrative unit is to be given a key role in coordinating the work of state, local, and federal programs. In its area of operation, a regional development agency should be given primary responsibility to deal with the resources of the area as a unified whole. Selznick has summarized the grass roots ideology as follows:

> The place for the coordination of programs is in the field, away from the top offices which are preoccupied with jurisdictional disputes and organizational self-preservation. Coordination should be oriented to the job to be done, centering federal authority and its administrative skills and power upon special needs and problems of the area.[20]

In short, the ideology justified managerial autonomy, the cooperation and support of local governments, and administrative control coextensive with the natural unity of a region for resource development. The net effect of the ideology was to justify independence from federal control on the one hand while assuring regional support on the other.

The dual realities of organizational dependence on local groups and of the drive for autonomy were reconciled in the grass roots ideology through a variety of specific devices, including an extensive network of citizen advisory groups. Rather than serving as a vehicle for the development of participatory values, however, these associations more often than not were the local diffusers of hierarchical values. As Selznick notes,

> in many cases, perhaps in most, the initiation of local citizens associations comes from the top, and is tied to the pressing problem of administering a program. The need for uniformity in structure, for a channel through which directives, information, and reports will be readily disseminated; for the stimulation of a normally apathetic clientele; and for the swift dispatch of accumulated tasks.... Such associations...are commonly established *ad hoc,* sponsored by some particular agency. That agency is charged with a set of program responsibilities. These cannot be readily changed, nor can they be effectively delegated. As an administrative organization, the agency cannot

abandon the necessity for unity of command and continuity of policy—not only over time but down the hierarchy as well. What, therefore, can be the role of the coopted local association or committee?[21]

Faced with the necessity of mobilizing citizen support of administrative programs, while at the same time not being able to allow citizens thus mobilized to exercise substantial control over the content of programs, the TVA "educated" citizens so that they would accept TVA decision premises. The process of value diffusion by the TVA depended on positive rather than negative sanctions, as was the case of welfare policy noted earlier.

The extensive network of local voluntary associations provided free fertilizer to farmers as part of a conservation effort. The formal requirement that application be made for fertilizer during community meetings necessarily placed the farmers in a position of publicly acknowledging their indebtedness to the TVA-sponsored agricultural extension agents. This indebtedness had the effect of creating a sense of subordination among small farmers in the area.

As was pointed out in chapter 2, the power of bureaucracies depends importantly on its ability to provide benefits and meet needs. In the case of the TVA, the benefits were used as incentives to gain public acceptance of the TVA's substantive conception of planning and development in the Tennessee Valley and to reduce the hostility of farmers forced to move because of dam and reservoir development. A somewhat more implicit but nevertheless important consequence was to secure popular approval of the idea that it was proper to be subordinate to the expertise of TVA agricultural extension agents.

Modeling and instrumental training by primary institutions facilitate the diffusion of hierarchy, specialization, and impersonality. It has been suggested that the particular emphasis given to these values seems to depend on where the primary institutions intersect with bureaucratic institutions. Middle-class parents emphasize independence and false personalism in child-rearing while lower class parents tend to convey the importance of following commands and the acceptance of dependence. Schools tend to reinforce these values by modeling the collegial pattern of corporate organization to children in middle class neighborhoods, the factory being the school model in lower class neighborhoods. The polity manipulates models and patterns of reinforcement through public policy and relatedly through the program ideologies of public organizations.

4

Diffusion in Industrial
and Postindustrial Societies

THE ULTIMATE SOURCE of legitimate bureaucratic power is the capacity to provide something valued. Insofar as a bureaucracy is able to satisfy values and significant reciprocation is not possible, subordination must be offered. Dependence is particularly great where workers are not willing to resort to force, have few alternatives to their current employment, and feel they cannot do without the wages and other benefits supplied. Unwillingness to ignore the benefits offered is a key condition of submission and control. Bureaucratic benefits are likely to be regarded as indispensable when bureaucratic values are diffused to the family, school, and polity. Bureaucratic power is linked to personal development because the values of bureaucracies may not be consistent with the needs of the individual. Thus, if one accepts bureaucratic values because of the influence of "bureaucratized" socialization agents, one may be denied needs such as affection and autonomy.

The complexity involved in understanding bureaucratic power derives in part from the variety of values that must be served within the bureaucratic context. Added to this is the evolution of bureaucratic values and needs associated with changes in methods of production, technology, and social control. The meaning of bureaucracy for those in given social positions and for the vitality of primary institutions has varied with particular stages of bureaucratic development.

Two periods in the development of bureaucracies and bureaucratic values are quite clear. The first period, 1750 to 1850, marked the early development of industrialism at the expense of agricultural interests. During this period there developed the widespread expectation of continuous material advancement. The second period, 1850 to 1950, was one in which industry was bureaucratized; it was a period in which the emphasis on hierarchy, specialization of task, and impersonality reached its peak. A third and less well defined period, sometimes called the "postindustrial period" (beginning about 1950), is one in which the emphasis on task specialization and impersonalism is transformed because of changed demands of production. In the following section we shall provide greater detail on the changing content of the bureaucratic values and on their roots in the requirements of production characteristic of the period's industrial development.

EMERGING ENTREPRENEURIAL CONTROL: 1750–1850

During the late eighteenth and early nineteenth centuries, industrial entrepreneurs in England began to make major efforts to obtain political and cultural recognition. Reinhard Bendix[1] has noted that these entrepreneurs, representing a new type of production, had to overcome the resistance of established agrarian groups with vested interests in the older social, political, and economic order. Many early entrepreneurs, though not a majority, came from modest family backgrounds.

In a survey of 132 industrialists selected for their prominence in manufacturing during the period of 1750-1850, Bendix found that about one-third came from families of workers and small-scale farmers, whereas two-thirds came from families already established in business.[2] Bendix does not believe that entrepreneurs from the lower classes were "mere operatives or yeomen." By and large, industrialists coming from the lower classes had their origins in the crafts.

> This is not to deny that...men who did establish themselves were raised by their own efforts — commencing in a humble way, and pushing their advance by a series of unceasing exertions, having very limited capital to begin with, or even none at all save that of their own labor.[3]

The craft origin of a substantial proportion of the early entrepreneurs was carried forward in their attitudes toward education. In contemporary society the normal expectation is that the children of the newly wealthy will insist on higher education for their children, but this apparently was not the case for the early industrialists. Bendix, quoting Robert Owen, describes the early textile manufacturers as "plodding men of business, with little knowledge and limited ideas except in their own immediate circle of occupation."[4] When an established industrial family did send a son to the university, it was to enhance the social position of the family, and it was generally recognized that the son would not follow an industrial career.

The universities, much to the regret of the emerging entrepreneurs, were not places where the young would learn the skills necessary for conducting the operations of manufacturing enterprises or acquire the skills necessary for technical innovation. Insofar as technological development was an organized activity, it took place in independent societies for the encouragement of invention and technology.

The transition to industrial production was of course not without meaning for peasants and workers. "Several students of the period have pointed to the contrast between the work

habits indispensable in a factory and the work habits characteristic of the peasant household or the household workshops of
the putting-out system."⁵ Peasants, when they were attached to
the land, had erratic schedules. The summer was characterized
by long hours of work. During the winter, when the daylight
hours were short and the fields were fallow, time was taken up
by the "putting-out system," or what otherwise has been called
the household industries system. But even here the industrial
notion that work should have regular hours throughout the
year was not a part of accepted belief. The usual pattern in
household industry was extremely long hours of work or long
periods of idleness. A reason for the irregularity of work in the
household industries was the uneven demand for goods.

One of the major problems faced by the new entrepreneurs
was to assure an adequate supply of factory labor, for peasants
were reluctant to leave their traditional occupations in the
countryside. Also, peasants were reluctant to join in the routine
working schedules necessary for factory work. Initially these
problems were resolved by emphasizing family labor; later they
were resolved through child and female labor.

It was not unusual in the early industrial period for an entire
family to enter the employment of a single factory, with the
father supervising the work of wife and children. This may
seem a bit unusual from a contemporary perspective, but it was
a natural carryover from the pattern of employment that pre-
ceded the factory system. The father was the task leader for the
family in agriculture and household production. The special
position of the father vis-à-vis his family in the factory was not
to last long, however. The demands of technology and the
market for labor worked initially toward displacing the father
as a managerial figure and eventually toward removing him
altogether from factory employment.

Women and children were a suitable work force for early
machine technology. Much more than men of peasant origins,
they were likely to take a submissive attitude toward supervisors

and to accept the high degree of specialization and routinization of factory work. The massive presence of women and children in the factory was a major influence, in turn, on the general attitude of early industrialists toward their workers.

Entrepreneurial Ideology

The dominant entrepreneurial ideology held that the poverty of workers was the result of their improvidence. "Long hours, poor health conditions, cruel exploitation of children, low wages, and all similar conditions could be explained or justified, if need be, if the source of all misery was the improvidence of the laboring people."[6] The improvidence of factory workers was tied to the notion that poverty was inevitable or avoidable in some cases only through the efforts of the workers themselves in restraining the growth of family size.

Malthus's idea that the population would inevitably live at the subsistence level was central to this ideology. The alleged inevitability of poverty was attributed to the tendency of the population to expand in proportion to the size of the food supply. This implied that the size of the working-class family would expand in proportion to the expansion of wages. Thus, if a working-class family was to improve its standard of living, it had to be through limiting the size of the family, a matter not subject to control by industrialists and therefore a matter beyond their responsibility.

While it was generally understood among the early entrepreneurs that the basic economic condition of the workers would of necessity be at the subsistence level, there was also the understanding, rooted in agricultural and guild traditions, that factory owners had an obligation to "look after" worker subsistence and morality. Paternalism was a two-edged sword because, while it may have guaranteed subsistence, it also was a vehicle to inculcate values conducive to entrepreneurial control and worker subordination. A variety of specific devices were developed for this purpose.

"In-kind" remuneration rather than wages was common. For example, workers were provided plots of ground for growing food or were allowed to keep cattle in return for deductions from wages. These sorts of arrangements extended to housing, clothing, and even meals. There is little doubt that this system of compensation increased the dependence of the workers on the owners, although the motives of the owners varied from the crass desire to create economic dependence to a sincere desire to insure minimal needs.

The emphasis on paternalism was the product of agrarian and guild traditions. Decentralization of worker control through the worker subcontracting system reduced the importance of these traditions.

> Merchants and manufacturers frequently did not deal with their workers directly, but through various middlemen.... The recruitment and management of labor were often left in the hands of masters, foremen, subcontractors, and others, for reasons of technology and organization. This delegation of all control over the workers to a variety of middlemen was not confined to the putting-out system, but prevailed in many industries in which the workers had already been gathered under one "roof."[7]

The decentralized control of workers had several important consequences. It was a significant factor in undermining the older tradition of paternalism by owners toward workers. The intentions of the owners cannot be clearly understood at this time, but it is probably fair to say that the subcontracting system allowed the owners to treat workers impersonally because they were not directly in control of wages and working conditions. The system also allowed the subcontractors to avoid responsibility for the conditions of the workers because the temporary nature of contracts with industrial owners required that they develop instrumental relations with their workers. In the initial period of the system, it was common for the subcontractors to exploit their own craft status. In the preindustrial period it was generally expected that master artisans would be responsible for apprentice subsistence needs such as food and lodging. The pressures of the industrial subcontracting system, however, meant that while labor subcontractors may have conveyed the impression that they would protect subordinate interests, this was not often realized.

The very survival of workers was threatened when the buffer provided by owner paternalism became less important in worker-owner relations. One result of this threat was the emergence of collective worker protests.

In the early 1800s agitation was particularly strong against the "corn laws," which placed a heavy tax on food, and against laws that prevented the nonlanded working class from voting and from organizing collectively to protect its economic interests. By 1826 the working class was sufficiently organized to force abolition of the laws that prevented workers from organizing to bargain with their employers. Industry was also faced with increasing frustrations and economic losses due to import tariffs on materials necessary for manufacture. In response to these developments, a modified entrepreneurial ideology developed that attempted to cement the interests of the working class and the entrepreneurs against the now fading agrarian aristocracy. This ideology is captured in a campaign speech by John Bright, a mid-1800s industrialist.

> I am a working man as much as you. My father was as poor as any man in this crowd. He was of your own body, entirely. He boasts not nor do I of birth, nor of great family distinctions. What he has made he has made by his own industry and successful commerce. What I have comes from him, and from my own exertions.... I come before you as a friend of my own class and order; as one of the people.[8]

In this single paragraph Bright captured the essence of the new entrepreneurial ideology that emphasized individual achievement and responsibility. By this doctrine, the working class was no longer condemned to subsistence levels of existence. By hard work and saving, even the humblest were capable of great success. Although somewhat perverted, the notion of equality implicit in the emphasis on achievement had widespread appeal. All persons, whatever their social origins, were capable of material success. Definite limitations were placed, however, on the type of effort regarded as legitimate.

Savings and hard work were the accepted vehicles, whereas collective action by workers was specifically and vocally denounced. John Bright spoke highly of the working class's potential for success, but he roundly condemned the emerging tendency toward trade-unionism. The basic critique of unionism was that it was unnecessary for hard workers because they would reap the rewards of their productivity. It was also argued that unions were socially irresponsible because they were not committed to increasing productivity.

In the one hundred years between 1750 and 1850, British industry was transformed from a struggling mode of production into one that dominated major political and economic institutions. This transformation was paralleled by a major transformation in the values that were diffused to workers and the larger society. The values of paternalism and dependence were replaced by laissez-faire individual achievement for both owners and workers. By the middle of the 1800s the values of individual achievement and material success for the worthy were well established.

Significantly, the values diffused in this early period pertained almost wholly to workers and owners. Little attention was paid to management. This neglect was largely a consequence of the relatively simple management and organization problems implied by production techniques of the period. Complex hierarchies of authority and supervision, detailed rules and procedures, and the accompanying development of management as a distinct occupation did not begin until the middle of the nineteenth century.

GROWTH OF ADMINISTRATION, 1850–1950

Beginning about 1850, many Western countries experienced dramatic growth in the proportion of employees in administrative as compared to production positions (see figure 4.1). While there were substantial differences between countries in the proportion of the work force in administrative positions, the trend toward increasing proportions in administrative positions was unmistakable.

FIG. 4.1. RATIOS OF ADMINISTRATIVE AND PRODUCTION EMPLOYEES FOR FIVE COUNTRIES IN SELECTED YEARS.

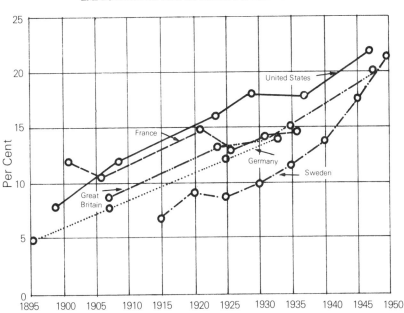

Source: Reinhard Bendix, *Work and Authority in Industry* (New York: Harper and Row, 1963), p. 216. Reprinted by permission of the author.

The relative growth in the number of administrators compared to persons in production positions was due largely to the displacement of production workers by machines. Increasingly, technologies were developed that cast people in the roles of controlling machines, specifying how machine products would be disposed of, and procuring necessary raw materials. The growth and concentration of capital goods in manufacturing industries was dramatic. For the United States, all machinery was worth less than $5 billion in 1879 in "constant" 1929 dollars. By 1899 the value of capital in manufacturing had tripled to nearly $19 billion (see table 4.1 for a more detailed tabulation of capital growth). In addition to the rapid growth in the total amount of capital used in manufacture, there is evidence of rapid capital concentration.

Earlier statistics are not available, but as early as 1918, 5 percent of all corporations in the United States produced 80 percent of corporate net income.[9] Much the same sort of picture emerges if one looks at total corporate sales in manufacturing. By 1901, of the largest 319 corporations, the four largest sellers of manufactured goods accounted for 33 percent of all sales. With this dramatic growth and concentration of capital and sales, it is not surprising that the pattern of employment also tended to become highly concentrated.

The average worker increasingly was employed in a work setting that was large in terms of the number of employees, the size of capital investment, and the scope of profits and sales. In 1904, 71 percent of all production workers were in corporate settings. By 1954 this already high proportion reached 90 percent. Indeed, as early as 1929 sole proprietorships, partnerships, and cooperative societies as a mode of industrial production were of historical significance only.[10]

Trends towards an increasing proportion of workers in administrative positions, a greater size of organizational units, and the growth and concentration of capital and profits had certain structural consequences that were of substantial importance for the content of bureaucratic values. Before the specific content of these values is examined, however, we must take a brief look at the structural consequences that accompanied these developments.

Systematic data on the patterns of internal change of organizations during the bureaucratic period of industrialization are not available, but there have been studies of a relatively large number of organizations differing in size in a single period of time. In the latter category is Peter Blau's study of 53 employment security agencies in 1968.[11] Blau's first major finding is that increasing organizational size "generates structural differentiation in organizations along various dimensions. The larger the number of employees, the more complex the organizational structure in terms of geographic decentralization, occupational specialization, hierarchical levels, organizational units at divisional headquarters, and sections within divisional units.[12]

TABLE 4.1.

TOTAL CAPITAL IN ALL MANUFACTURING
IN 1929 DOLLARS: 1879–1948.

Year	Total dollars (in millions)
1879	4,821
1889	11,157
1899	18,626
1904	23,295
1909	31,563
1914	36,737
1919	46,094
1929	63,292
1937	55,319
1948	77,982

Source: United States Bureau of the Census, *Historical Statistics of the United States: Colonial Times to 1957* (Washington, D.C., U.S. Government Printing Office, 1957), p. 412.

Increasing complexity and specialization in structural characteristics tend to reinforce the importance and size of the administrative as compared to the productive component of organizations. Specialization and complexity cause problems of communication and coordination. As an organization increases in
size, greater attention must be paid to making sure that
members of diversified units and occupational specialties
understand their roles in the productive process. The emergence
of these problems contributes directly to the increasing size of
the administrative component whose primary function is to
facilitate communication and coordination.[13]

The transformation of industrial production methods in the
bureaucratic period led to an emphasis on administration. It
also implied the development of a distinctive administrative role
style. In the earlier period of industrialism, unsophisticated and
rugged aggressiveness were idealized qualities. But capital concentration and organizational growth, with the attendant problems of communication and coordination, made this sort of individualism increasingly dysfunctional. The values surrounding
the administrative role, unlike those of the entrepreneurial role,
emphasized interpersonal skill and technical expertise. That administrators were increasingly influential and that they exhibited personal characteristics different from the earlier entrepreneurs is indicated by Bendix's historical analysis of the composition of American business elites.

Classification of over one thousand biographies of prominent businessmen between 1771 and 1920 shows the dramatic
growth of bureaucrats-administrators, the decline of
entrepreneurs-owners, and the growth of those who inherited
their positions of prominence and power in business (see table
4.2). The emerging administrative requirements of interpersonal skill and technical expertise are reflected in the educational backgrounds of these businessmen. In the bureaucratic
period of industrialism, the average educational level of prominent businessmen in entrepreneurial ownership positions remained relatively constant. But for the same period there was a

marked jump from 38 percent to 65 percent of bureaucrats having at least a college education. It is of course true that educational levels for the entire population, whatever their mode of employment, increased dramatically during this period. But even for the general population, those in bureaucratic work roles were more likely to be highly educated than those in non-bureaucratic roles.[14]

TABLE 4.2.

PERCENTAGE DISTRIBUTION OF AMERICAN BUSINESS ELITES
BY CAREER TYPE AND BY DATE OF BIRTH.*

Career Type	1771- 1800	1801- 1830	1831- 1860	1861- 1890	1891- 1920
Entrepreneurs	76	68	56	36	18
Bureaucrats	5	16	21	29	48
Heirs	19	16	23	35	34
Total Percent	100	100	100	100	100
N =	(121)	(75)	(332)	(344)	(131)
Not classifiable	(1)	(12)	(21)	(34)	(11)
Total N =	(122)	(87)	(353)	(378)	(142)

*Percentages based on classifiable cases.

Source: Based on Reinhard Bendix, *Work and Authority in Industry* (New York: Harper and Row, 1963), p. 229. Reprinted by permission of the author.

We have argued that interpersonal skill and technical expertise are two values that follow from the concentration and complexity of productive enterprise in the bureaucratic period. The logic for the emergence of these values is that the efficient and effective functioning of large bureaucratic enterprises requires interpersonal skill and technical expertise. It is important, however, to understand how the interests of the enterprise are understood by individual workers to be related to their own interests.

In the early period of industrialism, the personal interests of the entrepreneurs and workers were linked directly through profitability. Organizational profitability was alleged to be directly related to worker and owner income. More recently, it has been argued that managerial objectives may be much more complicated than simple profit maximization. The typical manager may be inclined to maximize sales subject to enough profit to satisfy stockholders' desire for dividends and also provide sufficient funds for financing future company growth. The desire to increase company sales and growth stems from the fact that executive salaries may be more closely tied to the scale of operations than to profitability.[15]

The emphasis on organizational growth and expansion is significant for bureaucratic values because it suggests a major transformation. With the growth and expansion of enterprises in the bureaucratic period, the entrepreneurial value placed on ownership is displaced by organizational mobility. Mobility is achieved by expanding the enterprise but also by movement up the organizational hierarchy. Organizational mobility ultimately displaces ownership as the accepted definition of success.

Organizational mobility quite literally means that one will regularly break friendships either because promotions require a physical move to a new plant location or because the social distance created by the promotion makes it increasingly difficult to maintain old affiliations and friendships. The Pahls, English sociologists, have uncovered some evidence that managers are very likely to experience physical mobility and that correlated with this mobility is a decline in the centrality of affiliation values. They found that 52 percent of those in commercial and administrative roles moved more than once every six years, whereas only 23 percent of those in technical and production roles moved more than once every six years.[16] Organizations expressed little concern about separation from family and friends. Nearly 45 percent of the sampled wives of moving managers said that "essential considerations" in a move were the character of the husbands' day-to-day activity at the new work site, pay, and advancement prospects; but only 5 percent were concerned with separation from family and friends.[17]

The orientation of managers toward nonwork needs for affiliation should not be confused with the managers' perception of the need for affiliation on the job. In the early 1960s, in the United States, the Brookings Institution asked a national sample of executives what they considered to be the worst and best features of any job. Twenty-one percent of the sample regarded the "ideal" occupation as one in which they could be around pleasant and agreeable people, while 27 percent stated that being around stimulating people was an essential part of an ideal occupation.[18] The nature of interpersonal relations was relatively less important to the nonmanagerial employed public; 10 percent fewer of this group saw these as aspects of the ideal job. While the evidence is not direct, one can infer that more of a manager's central life interests are related to work and that he or she therefore tends to "trade-off" meeting interpersonal needs outside of work for meeting them at work. Lower-level workers who experience lower levels of mobility are more inclined to meet interpersonal needs off the job.

By the middle of the twentieth century the bureaucratization of production was nearly complete. Production was concentrated in relatively few but very large enterprises with huge investments in capital goods. At the same time structural complexity increased, with an emphasis on the quality of organizational communications. The problems of production in the bureaucratic period also led to greater emphasis on white-collar occupations and on the specialized role of the manager. Indeed, some have argued that the manager displaced the owner as the major influence in bureaucratic operations. These technological and organizational changes had a significant impact on the content of bureaucratic values. The older emphasis on expertise became a requisite of all organizational roles, not simply that of the entrepreneur-owner. Beyond this, however, the indicator of success was transformed from ownership to organizational mobility. Interpersonal skills became central to bureaucratic functioning. Whereas in the earlier entrepreneurial period it was expected that affiliational needs would be met in the context of the extended family and friends, the pressure of mobility increasingly forced this need to be met on the job.

Bureaucratization deepened and broadened the psychological demands of work by requiring more complex expertise and also by increasing the range of needs one expected to satisfy at work. The fullest expression of the broadening of expected need satisfaction was not realized until the postindustrial period. In the postindustrial period the values expressed by bureaucratic institutions are so extensive that the effect is one of requiring nearly total personal involvement in the life of the organization. Production in the postindustrial period requires the internalization of not only competence-expertise values but also values relating to affiliation and esteem.

THE POSTINDUSTRIAL PERIOD: 1950 TO THE PRESENT

In the postindustrial period, planning is added to coordination as one of the central problems of enterprise. Rapid change requires the development of a capability to anticipate change so that productive resources can be rationally developed and deployed. Eric Trist has summarized some of the salient characteristics of the postindustrial society:

> The salient characteristic of the contemporary world is that it is becoming turbulent. This turbulence arises from the increased size of the total environment, the increased interdependence of the parts, and the unpredictable connections between them.[19]

Adaptation to change through the development of technology has always been a concern of industrial enterprise. But if Trist and other postindustrial theorists are correct, the extent of turbulence in contemporary industrial environments is unprecedented. Given the rapidity of change, an important question is: What sorts of organizational values are to be anticipated if enterprises are to adapt?

Warren Bennis has approached this question by suggesting that rapid and unexpected change makes the emphasis on hierarchy in organizations an outmoded value and that more emphasis must be given to "a change in managerial values toward more humanistic democratic practices."[20] However, the specific elements of the postindustrial organizational model emphasize a professionalized expertise rather than "humanistic democratic practices."

> Organizations of the future...will have some unique characteristics. They will be adaptive, rapidly changing temporary systems, organized around problems-to-be-solved by groups of relative strangers with diverse professional skills. The groups will be arranged on organic rather than mechanical models; they will evolve in response to problems rather than to programmed expectations. People will be evaluated not in a rigid vertical hierarchy according to rank and status, but flexibly, according to competence. Organizational charts will consist of project groups rather than stratified functional groups, as is now the case. Adaptive, problem-solving, temporary systems of diverse specialists, linked together by coordinating executives in an organic flux — this is the organizational form that will gradually replace bureaucracy.[21]

The professional is a model for the worker in the postindustrial organization. "Avarice," Bennis notes, is not the spirit of industry, particularly of professionals.

> Professionals tend to seek such rewards as full utilization of their talent and training and professional status...and opportunities for development and further learning. The main difference between the professional and the more conventional hourly employee is that the former will not yield "career authority" to the organization.[22]

An important value for the professional is success and mobility. But rather than that success and mobility being limited to a given organizational hierarchy, it exists within a professional hierarchy. The type of mobility implied by professionalism makes ever more central deep personal commitments to expertise and interpersonal skill. Since the idea of a career in a profession necessarily implies physical, social, and organizational mobility, interpersonal skills become crucial to one's capacity to transmit expertise in ever-changing social and organizational contexts.

A rough indicator of the extent to which the work force is becoming professionalized is the proportion of white-collar to blue-collar occupations. In 1900 in the United States, 18 percent of the work force was in white-collar occupations; by 1965 the proportion had increased to 45 percent. The proportion in manual and service occupations fluctuated between 45 percent and 50 percent, but farm workers dropped dramatically from 36 percent to 6 percent (see table 4.3).

Professionalization supports postindustrialism because acceptance of professional standards internalizes the control that in the bureaucratic period was the primary function of organizational hierarchy. The postindustrial era is distinguished from the bureaucratic period by the decline of hierarchical authority as a mechanism of coordination and control and the substitution for it of internalized professional norms.

A test of this argument would be to look at the depth and type of worker involvement in a period spanning the bureaucratic and postindustrial periods. Unfortunately this type of data does not exist, although it can be approximated by looking at contemporary organizations located on different parts of the bureaucratic/postindustrial continuum. Professor Tannenbaum and colleagues in Italy, Austria, Yugoslavia, and Israel compared large, complex plants with smaller, less complex plants in their respective countries in terms of the extent and type of worker involvement as well as the roots of involvement. The researchers asked workers in five countries, including the United States, "How much satisfaction do you get from your job in the plant compared to what you can do after leaving the

TABLE 4.3.
MAJOR OCCUPATION GROUPS, 1900 TO 1965 (IN THOUSANDS).

	1900	1910	1920	1930	1940	1950	1960	1965
White collar	5,115	7,962	10,529	14,320	16,082	21,601	28,726	32,104
	18%	21%	25%	29%	31%	37%	43%	45%
Manual and service	13,027	17,797	20,287	24,044	26,666	30,445	32,560	35,808
	45%	48%	48%	49%	51%	52%	49%	50%
Farmworkers	10,888	11,533	11,390	10,321	8,995	6,953	5,395	4,265
	36%	31%	27%	21%	17%	12%	8%	6%
Total	29,030	37,291	42,206	48,686	51,742	58,999	66,681	72,179

Sources: U.S. Bureau of the Census, *Statistical Abstract of the United States: 1968* (Washington, D.C.: U.S. Government Printing Office, 1968); U.S. Bureau of the Census, *Historical Statistics of the United States* (Washington, D.C.: U.S. Government Printing Office, 1956), p. 74.

plant?" Two things are interesting about the results. The first is that for all countries, whether the plants are large or small, the workers are inclined to say that work experiences are generally more satisfying than nonwork experiences. The second is that workers in the larger plants are more inclined to rate their jobs as satisfying compared to nonjob sources of satisfaction.[23] These findings provide tentative support for the notion that the larger, more technically sophisticated enterprises are characterized by a work force that is, relative to nonwork involvements, highly committed.

Significantly, the character of the work itself—how interesting and varied it is, how much opportunity there is to learn—is the most important determinant of work satisfaction and involvement. Very close to the importance of the type of work in determining job satisfaction is the amount of worker authority and influence; the more one has, the higher the satisfaction. Given the importance placed on interesting work and influence, it is easier to understand why upward mobility is such a central value. In those countries where influence in the enterprise tends to be highly hierarchical, as in the United States and Austria, worker satisfaction tends to be much higher at the top of the organization than at the lower levels. Also, there tends to be greater pressure for upward mobility in these hierarchical organizations. For example, it was found that in the United States 85 percent of the respondents were willing to accept added responsibility in exchange for promotion, whereas in the more equalitarian plants in Yugoslavia only 47 percent were willing to accept the additional responsibility.[24] The results are more dramatic when several additional factors are added to the analysis of what workers would be willing to accept in return for promotion. In the American plants 62 percent of the respondents said that they would accept frequent criticism from fellow workers, increased "worries," and the need for additional training if they were promoted. In the Yugoslav plants, the highest proportion willing to undergo these sacrifices for promotion was 43 percent.[25] Consistent with the previously cited data, workers in the larger plants in all countries were much more promotion oriented than those at the smaller plants. Approximately 20 percent fewer workers in the small plants were willing to accept the obligations and criticisms from coworkers attendant on promotion.[26]

The general picture that emerges from the cross-national Tannenbaum research is that workers in large enterprises see upward mobility in the organization as providing rewards meriting substantial sacrifices. Interesting work and influence are the substantive rewards of success. As significant is the finding that while these rewards are hierarchically distributed, the level of involvement in large plants is high, whatever the hierarchical position of the worker.

To this point we have spoken generally about level of involvement. It is also important to speak more specifically about the qualitative dimensions of involvement. That is, from the perspective of the workers, what is required in order for them to be successful in their drive for upward mobility and the rewards attendant on success? Tannenbaum asked workers, "How important are...the following factors for getting ahead in this company?" In response to a list supplied by the researchers, two major clusters of factors emerged. For the plants in the United States, there was a heavy emphasis both on the quality of task performance and on having outstanding ability to work with people. The interpersonal and skill requirements, at least as they are viewed by workers, are lower for all items in smaller plants.[27] Again, the data suggest that one of the major differences between the larger, more technically developed enterprises and the smaller enterprises is that in the former the level of commitment and expected performance is generally higher.

We have been concerned with how bureaucratic values have evolved since the early industrialization of England. Throughout this two-hundred-year period there has been a substantial emphasis on expertise and hierarchy, but the substantive definition of these values have changed. In broad summary, there has been an intensification of the emphasis on expertise through a new emphasis on interpersonal skill, and a broadening of the definition of hierarchy to include mobility in a profession. An important consequence of this broadening and intensification has been an increase in the level of commitment demanded and received by work organizations.

5

Models of Primary Institutions

BUREAUCRATIC POWER IS a central fact in the recognition and satisfaction of personal needs. To this point we have explored the conditions likely to lead to the dominance of bureaucratic values, and discussed in detail the primary institutional and social processes that diffuse bureaucratic values to individuals. Family, school, and polity promote the process of value diffusion by serving as basic agents of socialization. It is also true, nevertheless, that these agents of socialization often subject the individual to conflicting experiences and value demands.

In this chapter we shall be more explicit about the forms that these agents can take and the consequences of such forms for personal development. The family, school, and polity are institutional contexts for experiences vital for meeting deprivation and higher needs. It is here that a central question of this chapter emerges: in the most "ideal" or abstract terms, what would be the form of the family, school, and political community if they were to maximize the satisfaction of these needs?

In terms of their structure, internal processes, and interactions with one another, we are asking, what would those institutions look like? What sort of conditions would we expect to observe if need maximization were the principal goal around which they were organized?

How do we start discussing an ideal family or school without positing definitions so abstracted from the world that the discussion appears arbitrary, unreal, or irrelevant? Our answer to this question begins with the assumption that our notions about ideal institutions are rooted in observations about how institutions work in the real world.

We shall be concerned with the potential impact of each primary institution on the individual and with how they interact with one another. The ultimate consequences of those family forms that, for example, emphasize love, affection, and community bonds must be judged not only in terms of their direct impact on the individual as a child but also in terms of the longer run consequences of these experiences for development in school and work. Specification of ideal models will provide the criteria for evaluating the actual forms of these institutions, a matter developed in chapters 6 through 8.

DEMOCRATIC AND ELITIST MODELS OF THE POLITY

Whatever the particular form of a polity, it must deal with the problem of establishing major societal goals and must establish mechanisms for working toward their attainment. In discussing the role of the political system in bureaucratic diffusion, it was noted that it is an important transmitter of basic values to the citizenry. But the impact of the political system on the individual goes much beyond value socialization. Social policy and goals sanctioned by the political system include such matters as: the regulation of public conduct, as in the criminal law; the facilitation of certain kinds of activity, as in the provision of free health information; and the provision of direct services, such as therapy for the disabled. While all political systems must somehow deal with these and other public problems, crucial differences exist in the processes for developing public goals on these issues, in the priority given to one or another type of public problem, and in the distribution of policy benefits to the citizenry. Substantial differences exist in the way in which political systems attempt to propel citizens up the hierarchy of needs, and in the selection of those whose needs are emphasized through public policy.

A major distinction is made between democratic and elitist political systems. Elitist systems tend to emphasize the role of a relatively small minority in key public policy decisions. Democratic systems emphasize processes that maximize the opportunity of citizens to set public policy. John Dewey stated the democratic principle when he wrote that the keynote of democracy as a way of life may be expressed as the necessity for the participation of every mature human being in the formation of the policies that regulate people living together.

From a democratic perspective, participation may or may not lead to more efficient decisions. Some people believe that a large number of minds are more effective in making decisions than a few. But the evidence is mixed. Whether mass participation leads to more effective decisions depends a great deal on the kind of issue involved. If the issue requires the application of imagination or the creation of innovative approaches, some type of collective decision-making process is more likely to yield a good result. But for certain types of routine problems, where a well-established technology exists, decisions by a well-informed few may be superior. From the democratic point of view, however, a benevolent and intelligent elite is unacceptable, even if it is willing and able to assure efficient decisions and material security. It is unacceptable because the sense of dependency created by the lack of participation stifles self-development. Relatedly, the democratic view holds that it is not possible or desirable to value the worth of one citizen over another in terms of the right of personal development. While some citizens may be more knowledgeable and intelligent than others, each has an equal right to personal development.

The elitist perspective is well summarized by Gaetano Mosca.

> In all societies — from those that are very undeveloped and have barely crossed the threshold of civilization, down to the most advanced and powerful societies — two classes of people appear: the rulers and the ruled. The first class, always the less numerous, has a monopoly on political power and functions, and enjoys the advantages that follow. The second, and more numerous class, is directed and controlled by the first in a manner that is more or less legal, arbitrary, and violent.[1]

Mosca's work is offered as a description of the essential character of all political systems. He does not provide an ideal model of how governments should function, which is our concern. Others, however, have taken Mosca's descriptive model of the political system and elevated it to an ideal.

Rule by elites is considered proper because its members are regarded as more competent than ordinary citizens to make policy decisions. Given substantial differences in the moral and intellectual quality of citizens, it is desirable that the best make public policy. Mass participation is discouraged by elitists. Provision for the selection of political representatives through elections is accepted. But participation in elections is not treated as an end in itself; its basic function is to assure that elites do not ignore the legitimate needs of the masses. Other mechanisms such as competition among elites and provision for mobility from a position in the masses to one in the elite are also elements of the elitist model. But, again, their purpose is to assure that elites rule in the interests of the masses, not to provide for mass participation as such.

These two models of the political system, one emphasizing equal and universal participation, the other limited participation and efficient decisions, imply different yet overlapping social conditions. The democratic view emphasizes the creation of a society in which all major social institutions support individual development through participation. It requires that there be popular participation not only in political decisions but also in the workplace, school, and family.

In the democratic view, an intimate linkage between the political system and other social institutions is required because the capacity to participate in the political system assumes training. This training is thought to include but also to go beyond the formal routines of civics classes in schools. It is implied in the character of intense family, school, and work relations. In short, all major institutions, at their best, are social-psychological launching pads for participatory involvement in the political system. It is well established in political science literature that the feeling that one's actions (such as voting and writing letters to officials) will have an impact on public policy is an essential precondition of political participation. The feeling that one's actions will make little difference (viz., a lack of political efficacy) means that the likelihood of participation is substantially reduced.

The family, Renshon[2] has found, is an important element in the development of a sense of political efficacy. Development of this sense requires that the individual confront and master a variety of situations. Each successful act of mastery increases the belief that what one does makes a difference—that control can be extended over one's life. If parents rigidly control their children and thereby fail to provide opportunities for success (and failure), there is limited opportunity to develop a sense of personal efficacy. The results are similar to authoritarian restrictions imposed by parents who tend to overprotect their children, screening them from situations that the parents fear or find anxiety producing. Feelings of personal control and efficacy, initially developed in the family, can be generalized at a later time to the political system. It is for this reason that democratic theorists are so vitally concerned with the functioning of the family.

The quality of participation in the political system is also affected by the educational system. Education is important because it transmits basic knowledge about the workings of the political system. It is also responsible for developing psychological perspectives that will either inhibit or encourage democratic involvement. More highly educated persons exceed the less well educated in such matters as awareness of the impact of government on individuals, command of political information, scope of political opinion, likelihood of engaging in political discussion, diversity of people with whom political discussion is carried on, and belief in the helpfulness and trustworthiness of others.[3]

The social focus of the elitist model is more specialized. As we have indicated, key policy decisions are thought best limited to the most intelligent, educated, and moral. The participative character of the school tends to be regarded as a private and separate matter largely unrelated to the proper functioning of the political system. The elitist perspective, however, does not ignore the impact of the family and school because it must assure that there will be mass acceptance of elite rule and that elites will govern in the interests of the masses. A clue to the proper role for the family and school, from the elitist perspective, is embodied in Dye and Zeigler's position that

> to believe that making American government more accessible to mass influence will make it any more humane is to go directly against the historical and social science evidence. It is the irony of democracy that masses, not elites, pose the greatest threat to the survival of democratic values.[4]

From the elite perspective, a central challenge to the political system is how to protect elite minorities from the excesses and injustices of majorities. "James Madison warned," say Dye and Zeigler, "that protection against majority oppression 'is the real object to which our inquiries are directed.'... The question is not how to control elites, but how to restrain the masses."[5]

Two essential elements in the elitist strategy for restraining the masses are maintaining elite legitimacy and encouraging the development of local community and group identifications among the masses that focus their attention on local rather than national problems. The family and educational system play an important role in maintaining elite legitimacy because they can inculcate a sense of duty and obligation to superiors and public authorities. "It must be recognized that the schools inculcate the values of the political system and this inculcation must be deliberate, considered, and effective."[6]

Secondary associations also receive a great deal of attention by elite theorists. These intermediate groups, of which voluntary associations are a major example, help ensure that the mass citizenry will not be mobilized against elite minorities.

> People become available for mobilization...when they lack or lose independent group life.... The lack of autonomous relations generates widespread social alienation. Alienation heightens responsiveness to the appeal of mass movements because they provide occasions for expressions of resentment against what is, as well as promises of a totally different world. In short, people that are atomized readily become mobilized.[7]

The family and institutions such as the school, civic club, and community association prevent mass political mobilization and the emergence of political demands that destabilize political elites. High levels of political participation endanger stability by bringing in those who do not respect the rules or values of elitist governance. Seymour Lipset, for example, notes that

> the poorer strata everywhere are more liberal or leftist on economic issues; they favor more welfare state measures, higher wages, graduated income taxes, support of trade unions and so forth. But when liberalism is defined in noneconomic terms — as support of civil liberties, internationalism, and so forth — the correlation is reversed. The more well-to-do are more liberal; the poorer are more intolerant.[8]

This view of the masses is buttressed by the argument that lower-class culture is authoritarian, reflecting the uncertainty of the lower-class social world and the rigidity of its work environment. All of this is said to be reinforced by an educational system that emphasizes dependence and certainty rather than independence and tolerance for differences.

The elitist orientation is not friendly to forms of political participation that encourage the development of more democratic attitudes and personalities. Apathy and authoritarian attitudes are treated as mass characteristics not realistically subject to change. Little conflict is seen between the citizen's actuality and his or her potentiality; they are viewed as essentially the same.

By contrast, the democratic model sharply distinguishes actual citizen attitudes, values, and behaviors from potential characteristics. The absence of democratic attitudes is not regarded as inevitable; rather, it invites an analysis of the social and political conditions that induce these values and behaviors and a consideration of how these conditions might be changed. Attention is focused on alternative institutional arrangements that will enhance the ability of citizens to develop.

There are, then, fundamental differences between the elitist and democratic models of the political system. Democratic models are much more concerned with providing opportunities for citizen participation in public decisions. The emphasis on participation stems, in turn, from the commitment to encourage the development of human potential. Elitist systems, on the other hand, are primarily concerned with assuring that those who are in some sense the best will govern in the true interests of all. The democratic model is more congruent with personal development than the elitist model. The ability to conceive and attain personal goals, and participation in the making and implementation of public policy are major conditions of personal development.

CONDITIONS FOR INTIMACY IN THE FAMILY

From the elitist perspective, the family functions to preserve the stability of the political system by insulating elites from the masses. From the democratic perspective, the emphasis is on how the family prepares the young for responsible participation, the objective of which is not necessarily system stability but personal development. It is not surprising that these rival conceptions of family political roles presuppose substantially different models of family structure. One is usually described as democratic, the other as traditional. Skolnick has summarized the major differences in the socialization that characterizes these two major types (see figure 5.1). The traditional family is organized around obedience; the democratic family, around the personality of the child. The democratic family tends to inculcate values and behaviors that express individualism and autonomy, whereas traditional families tend to inculcate values and behaviors that express obedience and conformity.

The traditional family places much emphasis on differentiating roles played by mothers, fathers, and children. But this relatively strict division of labor and power is glued together by inculcating the belief that role and power differences are necessary for the survival of the family group. Heavy emphasis on rules and respect for authority thus serve to maintain the conventional social order of the family. Traditional family patterns occur with some regularity in the American working class. Urie Bronfenbrenner's review of studies on child socialization from 1932 to 1957 lead him to the conclusion that "the most consistent finding documented (in the area of techniques of discipline) is the more frequent use of physical punishment by working class parents. The middle class, in contrast, resort to reasoning, isolation, and...'love oriented' discipline techniques.[9]

Kohn[10] finds these differences in child-rearing patterns to be part of a more general tendency of working-class parents to value conformity over self-direction, while middle-class parents tend to value self-direction over conformity.

Differences in socialization practices to some extent parallel differences in family structure. Family structures may be

Fig. 5.1.

Two patterns of socialization.

Traditional or Status-Centered	Democratic or Person-Centered
1. Each member's place in the family is a function of age and sex status	1. Emphasis on selfhood and individuality of each member
2. Father is defined as boss and as agent of discipline; he receives "respect" and deference from mother and children	2. Father more affectionate, less authoritative; mother becomes more important as agent of discipline
3. Emphasis on overt acts—what a child does rather than why	3. Emphasis on motives and feelings—why a child does what she or he does
4. Valued qualities in a child are obedience, cleanliness	4. Valued qualities in a child are happiness, achievement, consideration, curiosity, self-control
5. Emphasis on "direct" discipline: physical punishment, scolding, threats	5. Discipline based on reasoning, isolation, guilt, threat of loss of love

(Figure 5.1 continued)

6.	Social consensus and solidarity in communication; emphasis on "we"	6.	Communication used to express individual experience and perspectives; emphasis on "I"
7.	Emphasis on communication from parent to child	7.	Emphasis on two-way communication between parent and child; parent open to persuasion
8.	Parent feels little need to justify demands to child; commands are to be followed "because I say so"	8.	Parent gives reasons for demands, e.g., not "shut up" but "please keep quiet or go into the other room, I'm trying to talk on the telephone"
9.	Emphasis on conforming to rules, respecting authority, maintaining conventional social order	9.	Emphasis on reason for rules; particular rules can be criticized in the name of "higher" rational or ethical principles
10.	Child may attain a strong sense of social identity at the cost of individuality, poor academic performance	10.	Child may attain strong sense of selfhood but have identity problems, guilt, alienation

Source: Arlene Skolnick, *The Intimate Environment: Exploring Marriage and the Family,* 2nd ed. Copyright ©1978, 1973 by Little, Brown and Co., Inc. Reprinted by permission.

arrayed along a continuum of extendedness. The least extended family is the nuclear family consisting of husband, wife, and children. At the opposite end of the continuum is the extended family consisting of blood relatives and their several related family units. This typology has been modified by Eugene Litwat, who identifies a third family type, the "modified extended family," which falls between the nuclear and extended types. The modified extended family consists of a coalition of nuclear families in a state of partial interdependence. Such partial interdependence means that nuclear family members exchange significant services with each other and also retain considerable autonomy (that is, they are not economically or geographically dependent).

The extended family is characterized in most cases by traditional socialization. Traditional socialization patterns are helpful in maintaining the relatively more complex structure of the extended family. The emphasis on age and sex differences and distinctive roles appropriate to these differences, provide a relatively specialized division of labor. The respect and deference received by the father from the mother and children assure that there will be an identifiable family head who will have the necessary power to integrate differential and specialized roles. The emphasis on conforming to rules and respecting authority serves to maintain the social order of the extended family in a similar fashion.

Since the nuclear family structure is much simpler, patterns of socialization are less concerned with the integration of specialized family roles. Less specialization is reflected in: father roles that are relatively more affectionate, mother roles that are relatively more concerned with discipline, and children and parents who are more likely to engage in two-way communication.

There is considerable debate over the desirability of the shift in the contemporary family from extended-traditional to nuclear and modified nuclear patterns. Dager has been vocal in questioning the effects of nuclear-family and modified-nuclear-family forms on the development of personality. He asks, "Do phone calls, sporadic visits, financial assistance, and prolonged physical presence only in dire circumstances provide the kind of atmosphere necessary for the facilitation of identification by the children of the new family?"[11] Dager suggests that normal occupational stress, together with stress coming from child rearing and community, must be faced in virtual isolation from those most able to provide emotional support and tension release, that is, members of the extended family. Dager contends that what is required to deal with these stresses is not the occasional face-to-face contact occasioned by major crises, but rather a continuous pattern of supportive contact.

Problems of familial inaccessibility are particularly acute when geographic distance is coupled with upward social and occupational mobility. For example, it has been found that upward mobility among married women tends to produce social isolation from the extended family and from neighbors.[12] Similarly, Rossi has found that the neighborhood in mobile areas is likely to be perceived as unfriendly and the residents as hesitant to form personal ties.[13] The major consequence of this isolation from agents of familial help is to force parents to turn to formal help agents such as baby sitters, nursery schools, early child care centers, schools, park and recreation programs, psychiatric and psychological counseling centers, social security, retirement plans, retirement homes, and welfare agencies.

A major implication of Dager's critique is that the nuclear family may threaten healthy personality development. The increasing complexity and impersonality of agents outside the family who raise children does not provide the child-adult bond necessary for identification. If this is not supplied by family members, it is not likely to be provided by others.[14] Feelings of affection and self-esteem are closely related to the family's capacity to provide continuing warm contact, a condition precedent to having the feeling of being loved. Stability of adult contact is also prerequisite in the sense that identification is necessary for the development of one's self-image and therefore of self-esteem. Family inaccessibility, mobility, and the delegation of child care—all characteristics of nuclear families—do not bode well for meeting needs of affection and self-esteem.

Discussion of the ability of the family for meeting needs must also address the satisfaction of material needs. It is not implausible to argue that the nuclear family is more congruent with an advancing bureaucratic and technological society, and is therefore better able to meet material needs. Thus, while the extended family may provide advantages in the need areas of love and esteem, these may be secured at the expense of material needs.

Bureaucratic power stems in part from the fact that bureaucracies allow people to better meet their material needs. It is the implicit recognition of this need-fulfilling capacity, reinforced by the diffusion of bureaucratic values, that significantly enhances bureaucratic power. Bureaucratic power is the subject of controversy, discussion, and analysis because in addition to its need-fulfilling capacity, it has direct and indirect tendencies through such institutions as the family to deprive individuals of other need satisfactions.

These tensions, conflicts, and apparently contradictory meanings of bureaucratic power for the family are to a certain extent paralleled in the political system. Elitist politics, at their best, are led by those who, in a technical and moral sense, are the worthiest and most intelligent. One of the major advantages claimed for elitist systems is that, owing to superior leadership, they are more likely than democratic systems to provide advanced levels of material attainment. The major response by those advocating democratic systems is not that democratic systems are necessarily better in providing "goods and services" to the citizenry, but that they provide better opportunities for the sort of participation necessary to personal development. There is no easy resolution of these tensions. As the following discussion will indicate, schooling seems also to have contradictory meanings for personal development.

FAMILY, BUREAUCRATIC, AND CORPORATE MODELS OF THE SCHOOL

Considerable attention has already been given to the school as a diffuser of bureaucratic values. It was noted that the factory and corporation are modeled by schools in order to provide children with a distinct and favorable picture of the industrial order. Factory schools have as their primary purpose the inculcation of values to the industrial working class, especially those concerned with increasing output of standardized products. The corporation school is designed to meet the needs of large bureaucracies, especially the needs of problem solving and innovation. In the factory school, specialization, hierarchy, and instrumentalism are modeled to the student by the narrow expertise of the teacher, the superior power position of the teacher, and the routinization of the student's schedule and work. The corporation school's emphasis on problem solving and innovation is manifested in collective decision making by both teachers and students and by complexity in the organization of the school and the students.

That the corporation and factory schools have different characteristics is clear. The factory school's emphases on routinization and hierarchical subordination is in sharp contrast to the corporate school's emphases on problem solving and collegial relationships. Both of these school types, however, ultimately share a commitment to bureaucratic organization and productivity. Schooling in the factory and corporate settings ultimately has been justified not so much in terms of the personal development of the student but rather in terms of increasing wealth and industrial output. The model that is clearly distinct from both the factory and corporation school is the family school.

The family school emphasizes the nurturing role of the teacher and the opportunity for exploration of new social and technical relationships. Grannis observes that the family school was instituted in New England in response to the failure of the extended family to fulfill certain functions in early American colonial society.[15] The colonial school reflected features of the colonial family in relationships with teachers and peers. Typically, a single class in a family school has a wide range of ages and the teacher is in substantial part a surrogate mother. The model of the family school was most explicitly developed by John Dewey:

> If we take an example from an ideal home, where the parent is intelligent enough to recognize what is best for the child, and is able to supply what is needed, we find the child learning through the social conversation and constitution of the family. There are certain points of interest and value to him in the conversation carried on: Statements are made, inquiries arise, topics are discussed, and the child continually learns. He states his experiences, his misconceptions are corrected. Again the child participates in the household occupations, and thereby gets habits of industry, order, and regard for the rights and ideas of others, and the fundamental habit of subordinating his activities to the general interest of the household. Participation in these household tasks becomes an opportunity for gaining knowledge. The ideal home would naturally have a workshop where the child could work out his constructive instincts. It would have a miniature laboratory in which his inquiries could be directed. The life of the child would extend out of doors to the garden, surrounding fields, and forests. He would have his excursions, his walks and talks, in which the larger world out of doors would open to him.
>
> Now, if we organize and generalize all of this, we have the ideal school. There is no mystery about it, no wonderful

discovery of pedagogy or educational theory. It is simply a question of doing systematically and in a large, intelligent, and competent way what for various reasons can be done in most households only in a comparatively meager and haphazard manner. In the first place the ideal home has to be enlarged. The child must be brought into contact with more children in order that there may be the freest and richest social life. Moreover, the occupations and relationships of the home environment are not especially selected for the growth of the child; the main object is something else, and what the child can get out of them is incidental. Hence the need of a school. In this school, the life of the child becomes the all-controlling aim. All the media necessary to further the growth of the child center there. Learning? Certainly, but living primarily and learning through and in relation to this living.[16]

Since the center of the process is the interests and needs of the child, the elements of standardization and routinization found in the factory school are absent. Substantial efforts are made to allow a wide variety of experiences, to allow the child to explore objects and experiences of personal interest. The role of the teacher is primarily one of providing emotional support to the student, rather than providing highly specialized expertise. The corporation school's emphasis on teacher specialization and collective decision making is largely absent. In England, where the family school is well established, Grannis notes that

> children...work spontaneously with all kinds of materials that have been provided for them: clay, wood, and tools, musical instruments, Dienes blocks and Cuisenaire rods, cooking equipment, pendulums, books, and on and on. They move freely about the classroom and work in the corridors and outside. Only at the beginning of the day do the children and the teacher sit together for "prayers" that often take the form of a little play or some other presentation. During the rest of the day the teacher meets the children individually or in small groups, as she encounters them working on various problems they have set for themselves or forms a small group for reading and discussion.[17]

The factory and corporation schools specifically seek to inculcate specialized knowledge and skills; the family school is much more concerned with personal and social integration. The factory and corporation schools are concerned that the student learn skills that will facilitate the performance of roles in industrial society. The family school, on the other hand, is not so much concerned with fitting students into available social slots as with providing them with the ability to utilize adult experiences for defining and meeting personal needs.

Understanding of the relationship between the type of school and personal development requires evaluation in the context of the larger society. For example, if the context is an industrialized economy, with its threats to the development of identity, it is likely that family-type schools would be particularly important for personal development. With its emphasis on emotional support and identity development, the family school provides the student with the capacity to integrate and make more meaningful the highly segmental experiences of adults in industrialized societies. Conversely, in traditional societies, which tend to provide adults with fewer specialized, segmental experiences, personal development might be better served by corporation-type schools. The corporation school's emphasis on problem solving and innovation would seem to complement the need of self-actualizing individuals to learn techniques for attaining goals once they have been established.

The family context is also important for evaluating the consequences of schools. Persons coming from extended family backgrounds, where self concepts and identity tend to be well developed, may be better served by schools that transmit the specialized skills necessary for material success in corporate and industrial settings. In effect, the family-school emphasis on self-development and integration may usefully overlap some functions performed by extended family structures. Indeed, as we shall show in the final section of this chapter, a comprehensive evaluation of the consequences of any type of institution requires that one consider its interaction with other types and kinds of institutions (i.e., extended family with corporate school, and democratic political system or nuclear family with family school and elitist political system).

Social Structure and Personal Development

Power is necessary for development because one must have the capacity to set and attain goals consistent with personal needs. A major social condition for the maintenance of individual power is the ability of basic institutions (family, school, political system) to express their distinctive core values. It is only when these institutions provide a diverse set of need-fulfilling opportunities that the individual is at some advantage in defining and fulfilling personal needs. When all institutions present similar values (i.e., bureaucratic), the ability to meet the individual's diverse needs is proportionately reduced. This discussion of power and development will now be made more specific. In particular, we shall examine the complex relationships between primary institutions and development.

Participatory premises lead one to conclude that development is best promoted by that model of family structure that optimizes democratic processes and values, in other words, the one that is most participative. Yet — and here the evidence from social science is mixed at best — a number of respected family scholars have concluded that the conditions of personal life that prevail in the traditional family are more apt than the democratic structure to encourage development. The apparent paradox can be resolved if one keeps in mind that one has a variety of needs and that primary institutions must in one way or another satisfy all of them. Thus, while traditional families imply values of hierarchy and subordination that are inconsistent with autonomy, these values may be relatively effective in providing emotional support and identification. In the context of work and school institutions that do not meet affective needs, the strengths of extended families recommend themselves very highly.

With regard to the relation of school structure, the issues are unfortunately no sharper or simpler than at the family level. The majority view is that the family-school structure, with its emphasis on self-growth, new experiences, social integration, and so on, is the most desirable. This is contrasted with the factory-school structure, whose chief function is to produce persons who will respect authority and the importance of specialized competence. Despite current talk about returning to fundamentals after an era of "progressive" education in the public schools, few teachers or parents are prepared to subordinate children's feelings and personalities to the acquisition of specialized knowledge. In this sense, the family school functions as a preferred model because it places the child's sentiments, feelings, and social adjustment at the center of educational theory and practice.

Does the emphasis on sentiments in the family school contribute significantly to development? Again the issue is one of context. Clearly, if families provide emotional support, the efforts of schools in this area are simply redundant. As we shall see, families increasingly do not provide for emotional needs; therefore it is to be expected that schools will attempt to respond to students' affective concerns. The family school is essential in the event of affective deprivation at home.

Schools are complex systems serving the very young to the very old. Therefore it is not satisfactory to prescribe a single type of school for all groups. Certainly, at the more advanced levels of the educational system, expertise must become central. Technical and analytical capacity are necessary to establish goals and work toward their fulfillment. From this perspective, good schools are those that emphasize the acquisition of objective knowledge. Bureaucratic and corporate schools, particularly at advanced levels, may be desirable if the hierarchy of authority is legitimized by competence and not by false personalism and tradition.

What is more important than consistently participative family and school institutions is the availability of diverse family and school environments. With such diversity, the deficiencies of one can be compensated for by the strengths of the other. This conclusion also suggests that consistent domination of family and school by bureaucratic values is detrimental.

The political system must be participative. We have been careful in discussion not to suggest that either of the political models may be consistent with personal development. The political system is the major institutional area in which mature adults have the opportunity to influence the establishment of goals. Participative schools and families admittedly can provide training, but in the end the child is by definition dependent. The political system, properly, can encourage the family and the school to meet deprivation needs, but it should not be structured in such a way that the meeting of deprivation needs is its major objective.

6

The Bureaucratization of the Family

IN EARLIER CHAPTERS we indicated that industrial development has heavily influenced structural and socialization patterns of the family. Extended family forms appear to be more conducive to satisfying needs than nuclear forms. We saw that the impact of family structure on family members is a function of the larger institutional context in which the family operates. Changes in that context may result in similar family structures having dissimilar consequences for the individual. Hence, the nuclear family may be "liberating" when intimate relations in school or work are maximized, but constrictive when those same institutions block the satisfaction of intimacy needs. Since institutional context is so important for an understanding of family impact, it is vital to examine the character of the family before and during the process of industrialization and bureaucratization. This aspect of analysis is important if we are to have confidence in our premise that industrialization and bureaucratization have been major forces in the transformation of the family.

Since personal development presupposes the prior satisfaction of needs, we must explore the following matters that place our understanding in an historical perspective:

1. How much of a parallel is there between evolving family and industrial structures?
2. To what extent does the contemporary structure of the family coincide with public expectations, and thereby indicate the diffusion of bureaucratic values and power?
3. What are the implications of our findings regarding family structure and popular attitudes for the prospects of meeting needs and providing the necessary family context for development?

THE CONTEMPORARY STRUCTURE
OF THE AMERICAN FAMILY

By the turn of the century only a relatively modest proportion of Americans lived with parents in an extended family setting. Indeed, by 1974 the extended family, with multiple nuclear families related by kinship ties living in the same household, was virtually nonexistent in the United States. By that year less than 2 percent of all American families lived in a household headed by a kin relative. Nonextended family living arrangements were also reflected in the decline in average household size. In 1900 the average number of people living in the same household was 4.76; by 1974 it had declined to 2.97.

If people are no longer living in extended households, what are their structural living arrangements? The answer seems to be that they are more frequently living alone or with one other person. The proportion of single-person households increased from 5.1 percent in 1900 to 17 percent in 1970. Two-person households have increased from 23.4 percent in 1900 to 28.8 percent in 1970. Large households (seven or more persons), on the other hand, dropped from 20.4 percent in 1900 to 5.1 percent in 1970. The decline of large households has been paralleled by the increasing popularity of both marriage and divorce. In 1920, of the approximately 74 million people in the United States, 60 percent were married. By 1965 the proportion married peaked at 71 percent, falling to 68 percent by 1974. These figures take into account changes in the proportion of the population of marriageable age. The historical movement to marriage was paralleled by an increasing percentage of divorces. In 1920, less than 1 percent of the population was divorced. By 1974 there had been a steady increase to nearly 5 percent.[1]

However impressive, these data on changes in the American family do not give adequate meaning or understanding of the consequences for the individual. As we suggested earlier, the meaning of family arrangements for the individual cannot be entirely determined by looking at the family alone. It must be understood in a larger institutional context. As social forces change, family arrangements may have substantially different meanings for the individual. Family structure has changed considerably over the past century. The dynamics of those changes are intimately tied up with the larger forces of the industrial society.

FAMILY AND HOUSEHOLD STRUCTURE IN TRANSITION

Reasonably reliable data on family size are available only since the turn of the century. Conclusions about family conditions before that time must be tentative. The best studies of preindustrial family structure have been conducted in England by Peter Laslett and his associates.[2] The Laslett research was concerned with the size and composition of households in England from 1564 to 1961. The major conclusion, challenging commonly held expectations, is that the mean size of households in England had not changed substantially between 1564 and 1900, although there was a substantial drop in household size after 1900. While there is some variation in the estimates, the range of household size in this period is between four and five members. Laslett observes that "It would seem...that mean household size did not change markedly between the pre-industrial social order in England, and that which succeeded it in the nineteenth century."[3]

Behind the constant household size, some significant changes in household composition took place. Eventually these were to have a profound impact on the meaning of the family for the individual. In preindustrial rural England, household composition was affected by economic pressures. Poorer families, unable to provide for their children, were anxious that they fill positions as servants in the households of the middle class. Lodgers were taken in by poorer families to supplement family income. The net effect of economic pressures was the progressive dilution of the family by servants and boarders, although the average number of people living in a household remained fairly constant.

The rise of the factory in the 1850s was associated with a strengthening rather than a weakening of the household as a kinship unit. Anderson has noted that as early as 1851 in Preston, England, there were signs of a decline in the servant class.

> Employment in the factories was not conditional on co-residence, and the opportunities it offered to the young made it difficult to recruit suitable children to domestic service. Most of the domestic servants were immigrants, and the main sources of recruitment were purely agricultural villages where the children, lacking much previous contact with industry, seem to have found service the easiest adaptation to urban life in a factory town, and seem to have been particularly sought after by the middle class.[4]

With the rise of the factory system, however, it became possible for whole families to move from agricultural to urban areas because employment could be offered to the entire family. It was not uncommon to decentralize hiring responsibility to foremen and journeymen. It was also part of accepted practice that vacant positions be offered to kin, including spouse and children. In the early period of English industrialism, a typical pattern was the father-husband acting as patriarch in the home and as supervisor in the factory.

Anderson has shown that in agricultural England of 1564 to 1821, approximately 70 percent of the households had one or two generations under the same roof. But in the industrial-urban center of Preston in 1851 the proportion was 75 percent,[5] a clear indication of the growth in family extendedness. Thus the movement from rural to urban centers of work appeared to be facilitative of family extendedness, not a threat to it. But there were short- and long-term costs attached to that movement. The short-term costs were employment uncertainties and the wrenching effects of movement from familiar to unfamiliar surroundings. The long-term cost was the triumph of industrial over family values.

The growth in family extendedness associated with early industrialization provides an example of the way bureaucratic power is exercised and diffused. The economic benefits of industrial employment to rural workers were clear. The prospect of better wages and having family members all working in the same general area apparently outweighed the stresses associated with physical mobility. It took literally generations for some of the negative consequences of the movement to urban centers to become clear. Radical transformations in family size, function, and nurturing capacity were probably unanticipated. It is probably also fair to speculate that industrialists were not looking at the long-term consequences of industrial expansion for the family. This is so not only because short-term management issues seem to crowd out long-term problems, but also because the eventual condition of family change, namely bureaucratization, was unknown and unanticipated. It was not until the late 1800s that family form and function began its rapid transformation. The role of industrialism and bureaucratization in this change is further illustrated by the experiences of those who emigrated to the United States and worked in American industry.

Industrial Transformation and the Immigrant Family

By the turn of the century, the American industrial labor force was composed largely of poorly educated immigrants or children of immigrants. The percent of foreign-born male employees in 1907-1908 ranged from 85 percent in the sugar refining industry to 34 percent in the boot and shoe industry. Conversely, the proportion of male employees who were native-born or of native parenthood was only 6 percent in the sugar industry and 43 percent in the boot and shoe industry.[6]

The presence of large numbers of immigrants initially facilitated the recruitment of labor to industry in several ways. The presence of immigrants was consistent with the age-old practice of the foremen directly recruiting workers. Kinship ties between the foreman and workers served as channels of communication and recruitment. But once workers were on the job, such kinship ties were used to reinforce the workers' commitment to the foreman and thus to organizational productivity.

> Because the unskilled worker seldom had a definite occupational goal, other than a higher income, the unskilled worker followed the line of least resistance in seeking employment. In practical terms this meant that community or kinship ties became paramount. The unskilled workers' contacts were with people whose common bonds were social rather than industrial in nature. As a result family ties, village acquaintanceships, and religious affiliation rather than a shared body of knowledge, work reputation or union membership became the prerequisites for an area or occupation.[7]

Dependence on the foreman facilitated quick recruitment of labor, but it also often resulted in poor matches of skill to task. Nepotism did not guarantee that the skills and personality of the persons recruited would be suited to their job. Mismatches between worker and task became increasingly likely, given the family-based recruitment system, for two general reasons. The late 1800s and early 1900s marked the beginning of a rapid increase both in the concentration of capital used in the productive process and in the complexity of technology. An increasing proportion of industrial resources was devoted to expensive and complicated machinery, and relatively less reliance was placed on using people as primary productive units. Technological elaboration of capital required that greater consideration be given to the worker's ability to understand and facilitate the operation of machines. Conversely, physical ability became less important as a predictor of the worker's contribution to productivity and profit.

An indication of the scale of the person-task mismatches is reflected in the rate of turnover in American industry. Nelson reports that as firms began to collect data on resignations and terminations, it became shockingly clear that labor turnover was detracting from the efficiency of production. For example,

> The Amoskeag Company...reported that in 1912 it hired 20,000 men and women to maintain a labor force of 16,000. In December of the same year 48 percent of the factory employees of the Ford Motor Company quit or were fired. Ninety-one southern textile mills hired 57,000 new employees in 1907 but had at no time more than 30,000 individuals on their payrolls. The problem of retaining a reasonably efficient work force prompted the manufacturers themselves to take a more positive role in the recruitment of labor which had direct implications for the family.[8]

Increasingly, labor was regarded as a contingency that had to be given top-level consideration so that adequate supply and quality would be assured for expanding industrial needs. Nelson has outlined some of the changes that affected the role of the foreman in Ford plants.

> The Ford Program consisted of three important measures. The first, introduced in late 1913, stripped the foremen of much of their remaining authority. It established seven classes of

workers, each with specific ranges of wage rates; it eliminated the foremen's power to discharge...and it gave the employment department...increased responsibility. In the future department heads rather than the foremen would requisition new workers and the employment department, by means of elaborate sets of forms, would determine which applicants were suitable.[9]

The response of industry had a dual thrust, one directed to intraorganizational administrative arrangements, the other to the family and the characteristics of its members. For the first time the personal characteristics of the worker became a direct continuing concern of the employer. This concern was expressed by the establishment of personnel departments, "sociological" departments, home visits, and attitudinal surveys. Under the old system, judgments about personal characteristics were somewhat within the control of the family in that the foreman acted not only as a representative of industry but also as a member of a family, thereby taking into account responsibilities for the entire extended family.

The immigrant family was directly threatened by the middle-class standards of sociological departments and by the loss of placement functions. By 1920, being a member of an extended family no longer provided competitive advantages in the job market. Significantly, immigration reached its peak and began to drop off by 1910, just 30 years after the beginning of rapid capital expansion (see table 6.1).

The extended family forms found among immigrants probably were not typical of those who could trace their ancestry to the earliest American settlers. However, it is now clear that significant internal changes have taken place in these groups and that they are related to changes in the industrial system.

Changes in Family Structures and Functions for Nonimmigrant American Families

The doubts that Laslett and others have raised about the existence of extended family arrangements in preindustrial

TABLE 6.1

IMMIGRANTS AND CAPITAL IN MANUFACTURING, 1860–1940.

Year	Immigrants	Capital (in millions)
1860	153,640	-NA-
1870	387,203	-NA-
1880	457,257	4,821 (1879 dollars)
1890	455,302	17,452 (1899 dollars)
1900	448,572	23,295 (1904 dollars)
1910	1,041,570	31,563 (1909 dollars)
1920	430,001	46,094 (1919 dollars)
1930	241,700	63,022 (1929 dollars)
1940	70,756	55,319 (1937 dollars)
1950	249,187	78,067 (1948 dollars)
1960	265,398	110,455 (1957 dollars)
1970	373,326	-NA-

Source: U.S. Bureau of the Census, *Historical Statistics of the United States, Colonial Times to 1970,* Series P123-176, C89-101, and P197-204 (Washington, D.C.: U.S. Government Printing Office, 1975).

England are equally strong for preindustrial America because of peculiar conditions associated with early immigration and the frontier. Early American colonists were overwhelmingly from the lower strata of northern and western Europe. This meant "they brought with them a tradition of personal choice in marriage."[10] The tradition of parental and extended family influence on mate selection was strong only in the upper classes of western Europe, where it was perceived that family and kin interests could be affected by alliances of kinship groups through marriage. Mate selection in the lower strata was more independent of parental influence because the implications of a marriage for the standing of the extended family was not a major concern. As a practical matter, furthermore, poorer families were less able to influence the choice of mates because they could not provide a dowry to fund the marriage contract.

Another major factor reducing the importance of extended families in the United States was the mobility characteristic of the American frontier. Mobility from Europe plus the mobility associated with the settlement of the frontier both served to weaken extended family ties and to place greater importance on the nuclear structure of the family. These factors tended to reinforce notions of romantic love as the primary basis of mate selection.

Although the evidence suggests that early American family life tended to be nuclear and based on personal choice, it was patriarchal rather than democratic.

> The father was the actual and legal head of the family, dominating the normative decision-making process. The female gave up legal title to any resources she brought into marriage; they became resources at her husband's disposal.... The wife's usual lot in the colonial family was to bear and care for the couple's children and, under difficult conditions, to supervise the household....
>
> Legally, the child was no better off than the wife. The father was entitled to his child's services, and he could demand that the child work for him without pay. If the child worked for an outsider, the father was entitled to his earnings.[11]

Family size probably remained fairly constant for those families that could trace their origins to the colonial period. But the mid-1800s, a period of rapid industrialization, was associated with radical transformation of the internal functioning of the family and in the definition of family roles. The primary issue in this period was the composition of family roles, socio-emotional experiences relating to them, and the bearing of these roles on personal development.

Internal Changes in Nonimmigrant Families

Under the best of conditions it is difficult to explore the more intimate aspects of family relations. These difficulties become nearly insurmountable when one attempts to take a historical view. An innovative attempt is a series of articles by Herman Lantz and his associates.[12] The Lantz group has reconstructed a picture of power patterns between husband and wife, the extent to which romantic love was important, motivations for marriage, and conflicts between parents and children, from themes appearing in popular magazines between 1741 and 1865. Their most recent research deals with the period 1850 to 1865. This period is important because it coincides with the onset of rapid industrialization in the United States. More importantly, it was the Civil War period, during which there arose vital questions about equal rights for blacks and women:

> There was a general questioning of the position and authority of the male. The interpretations of Marxist writings, along with the writings of utopian socialists, appeared in literary works and magazines. Utopian efforts sprang up in America during the period and some, such as the Oneida community...expounded spiritual, sexual, and economic equality.[13]

In comparison to earlier periods, there was much greater discussion of the propriety of male power in the family. Indeed, there were three times as many discussions of this sort from 1850 to 1865 as during the entire period between 1741 and 1849. There was also a shift from prescribing subtle female influence over the male to overt female power.

> From 1741 to 1825, discussions of female power were primarily restricted to the family environment and courtship situations. Female power in general or women's rights and influence outside the home were seldom discussed and rarely advocated.... After 1825, however, these issues and topics became more common. The taken-for-granted nature of traditional roles was challenged by a growing controversy over the rights and responsibilities of women in work outside the area of the family.[14]

The importance previously placed on cooperation between men and women in the context of patriarchy was replaced in the 1860s by an emphasis on overt female power.

Associated with more emphasis on the exercise of overt female power was an increase in the explicit recognition of family conflict between husband and wife as well as between parent and child. It seems to have been a period in which conflict involved a large variety of factors that cannot be readily distinguished from contemporary sources.

> Some conflict over domestic roles and finances was discussed by the magazine writers, but few distinct patterns emerge with respect to other specific situations of marital conflict. In fact, we were impressed by the variety of alleged causes for marital troubles (lack of communication, drinking, finances, personality conflicts, in-law problems, extramarital affairs) and the similarity of these themes to contemporary complaints and explanations of marital disruption.[15]

There is some evidence that the pattern of child-wife subordination to the patriarch was also ending, although it would be many years before the dominance of the father-husband would be substantially eroded.

The question in part begged by a description of these forces in family life is how they are related to events of an industrial-bureaucratic nature. We have focused on the 1850-1865 period because it marked the onset of rapid industrialization in the United States. But we can go beyond the simple coincidence of changes in the family and industrialization. With industrialization came direct female employment outside the home and related changes in family roles.

The Diffusion of Bureaucratic Roles to the American Family

One of the clearest changes in the relationship between the family and work is the increase of female workers in industry. Industrialism was associated with the massive incorporation of women into the labor force. In 1870, 13 percent of the labor force was female, but by 1970 it had steadily increased to approximately 42 percent. In the same period the proportion of the labor force in agricultural employment declined from 53 percent to 3.5 percent. When the percentage increase in female employment is compared to the percentage increase in non-agricultural employment, it seems likely that most of the growth in the female proportion of the labor force was in manufacturing (see table 6.2).

Manufacturing provided superior employment opportunities because of its greater emphasis on making decisions and processing information as opposed to agriculture's reliance on physical strength.

Scholars assumed that in earlier periods of industrialism, working mothers neglected important female duties. Female paid employment was thought to be incompatible with effective housekeeping and child care. It was assumed to result in personality damage to children. Employed mothers were accused of being responsible for juvenile delinquency, divorce, and mental illness among both mothers and children.[16] Not surprisingly, as the proportion of mothers in the work force increased, so did the acceptance of them in their working roles. A recent survey asked: "There has been a trend toward more women being employed outside the home than in the past.... Do you think this trend toward more women working is desirable or undesirable?" Approximately 60 percent of those under thirty-five years answered that the trend was favorable.[17] In a 1958 study Weiss and Samelson found that working mothers were more likely to mention some aspect of their job than they were to mention either housework or their role in the family as wife and mother as a central source of feelings of usefulness and importance.[18]

Along with the greater legitimacy of paid work roles for mothers, there has been a shift in the espoused values central to mothers. Among those women who are most highly committed to work, heavy emphasis is placed on achievement rather than on nurturance and affective support.

While research is far from adequate, there are indications that these shifts in values are more pronounced among the middle class than among the lower class. For the lower-class

Table 6.2

Percent increase in female and

manufacturing employment.

	Percent Increase — Female	Percent Increase — Manufacturing
1870 – 1880	1.6	3.4
1880 – 1890	2.1	5.2
1890 – 1900	1.4	3.5
1900 – 1910	4.6	3.2
1910 – 1920	2.4	6.8
1920 – 1930	3.6	4.2
1930 – 1940	2.7	2.7
1940 – 1950	5.5	6.4
1950 – 1960	5.8	5.8
1960 – 1970	2.9	3.0

Source: U.S. Bureau of the Census, *Historical Statistics of the United States* (Washington, D.C.: U.S. Government Printing Office, 1975), pp. 127-28.

mother, work has been and is a means to meet basic "deprivation" needs. The income from work is necessary to pay for basic housing, medical care, and food. For the middle-class mother, work's central meaning is less related to basic deprivation needs; it is seen more often as a vehicle to personal development. The orientation to higher needs on the part of middle-class women makes sense because their more basic needs are assured by family income and/or by their opportunity for obtaining high-paying professional positions.

Working women generally exercise more power in the family than nonworking women.[19] The research findings, however, tend to be most consistent within specific decisional areas. For example, working wives have relatively more power in financially related decisions. "The Detroit Area Study...showed that employed wives, compared with nonemployed wives, made significantly more major economic decisions (what car to buy, what house to choose, whether to buy insurance, and whether the wife should work)."[20] Interestingly, working mothers have more influence on decisions regarding family size and patterns of child rearing. In those few studies where non-working wives had more power, it tended to be exercised in areas circumscribed by the household, such as food and household maintenance.

The difference in power between working and nonworking wives is much greater in the lower class than for the middle class. A plausible explanation is that because economic deprivation is greater in lower-class families, the economic power of the working wife is relatively more important than in a family in which the husband can provide generously for economic needs without the wife's income.

Changes in mate power relations are consistent with changes in child rearing, or at least what was said to be desirable in child rearing. The preindustrial period in the United States saw the child as a young adult with a proper and relatively fixed place in the division of labor. Much of the child rearing literature emphasizes that the socially recognized period of childhood did not extend beyond four to seven years of age. In the childhood period, emphasis was placed on breaking the child's will and inculcating strict principles of proper behavior. Teaching the rules of proper behavior and providing appropriate role models was regarded as the major responsibility of the parent.

Emphasis on learning well-defined adult roles early in life was consistent with the relative absence of economic security in the preindustrial and early industrial periods. The problem of child rearing was to assure that the child would be able, early in life, to contribute to the basic food and shelter needs of the family. These traditional prescriptions for child rearing were nearly extinct by the end of the Civil War.[21]

In the post-Civil War period, when industrialism began to develop rapidly, greater emphasis was placed on encouraging independence, and less emphasis on strict rules and roles and on extending the legitimate period of dependence and childhood. Rather than role modeling as the primary method of child rearing, direct day-to-day involvement in child rearing became the idealized parent-child relationship. These changes are summarized by Miller and Swanson as follows:

> We have summarized the child rearing spirit in the slogans, "Do what seems natural in training your child," and "Be sure the child is ready before you urge him to acquire new skills." Corporal punishment was minimized, rigid schedules for feeding and toilet training were abandoned, weaning from the breast was tied more to the child's interests than to a schedule, and strict prohibitions on thumb-sucking and genital exploration abandoned.[22]

CHANGE IN THE FAMILY AND
THE SATISFACTION OF NEEDS

Dramatic changes in the structure and patterns of family interaction are coincident with the development of bureaucratic industrialism. Families have become more democratic and less patriarchal; they have become smaller, and more dependent on emotional closeness within the nuclear unit for integration and less dependent on hierarchical role definitions. Relatedly, the family has become much more integrated into the larger economy. Women not only participate at very high rates; they also adopt workplace values such as achievement and increasingly reject traditional child-rearing values like nurturing as their central commitment.

The acceptance of new roles by women is an indication of the success of bureaucratic value diffusion. That is, not only have the objective characteristics of families changed, but also there are substantial signs that these changes have been largely accepted. The limited information presented on women's new work and family roles does not of course automatically apply to all areas of family life, but we have seen little evidence of resistance to the massive changes that have been taking place. Given these changes in the structure and function of the family and the acceptance of them, the remaining question is the extent to which they are supportive of meeting human needs.

Family changes have facilitated meeting the economic needs of family members. The evidence of the integration of women into the work force has been reviewed. Because it is so well documented elsewhere, we need not review the data showing the great increases in family income in the industrial period. The question that does arise, however, is the extent to which the higher needs of parents and children are being met in the modern family in comparison to older, patriarchal, extended family forms.

There is no easy answer to this basic question, but it can be made more manageable if one assumes that the family is the only institution that is capable of meeting primary emotional needs. Schools, political systems, workplaces, day care centers, and the like are basically instrumental organizations with relatively specific purposes and therefore not well suited to providing affective and emotional support. This premise accepted, we can now ask: Are basic needs for love and affection being better or more poorly met by "bureaucratized" families?

In chapter 3 we presented analytic arguments dealing with the process of identification and socialization. These suggest that extended family forms are relatively more effective in providing for affective needs. More directly, it is clear that romance and love, as topics of public discussion and as major criteria for mate selection, became prominent only since the onset of bureaucratic industrialization. Before the 1850s, at least in the United States, status and wealth were the primary considerations in the selection of a spouse. We assume that romance and love entered public discussion because of a widespread and unfulfilled need. Needs that are satisfied, it seems to us, are much less prominent features of public discussion, debate, and public policymaking.

It is significant, and we think consistent with this conclusion, that the preindustrial period was one of relative poverty and also one that emphasized the importance of wealth and status in the selection of marriage partners. It can be argued that with industrialization, particularly during its bureaucratic phase, came relative wealth but also affective deprivation. Thus there occurred a shift in emphasis from wealth and status to affection as the central criterion for mate selection. This shift in public discussion is taken as an indicator of the relative ineffectiveness of the modern family as an agent for the provision of affective gratification. It should also be noted that the evidence on idealized patterns of child rearing suggests that meeting emotional needs became a matter of increasing public concern since the onset of industrialization in the United States. Somewhat troublesome, however, is the relationship between extendedness in family structures and the meeting of human needs.

Evidence has been presented which suggests that in England and the United States there had been little change in average household size until the 1920s. This means that structural changes did not occur until long after the onset of industrialism. One is tempted to argue that the public discussion of meeting emotional needs in the family anticipated the decline in family size. That is, the idealized form of child rearing and mate selection noted above was an indication that all was not well in terms of the family performing affective functions for its members. It can be argued that although it was more than half a century after the onset of industrialism in the United States that the size of the family began to contract, the quality of affective relations began to decline almost immediately.

Intermediate between the changes in the quality of family relations and size were changes in roles. The decline in patriarchy and the increased democratization of power relations did not start immediately after the onset of industrialism but were well established before the size of the family began to contract in the 1920s.

The Process of Exchange
Between the Family and Industry

In several places we have attempted to show how the development of industrialism influenced the structure and processes within the family. Significantly, the process seems parallel for the English peasant who emigrated to industrial centers and the southern European immigrant who came to the industrial centers of the United States. In both cases the basic drive seems to have been the maintenance of the material and emotional well-being of the family unit. Industrialization provided an improved standard of living and, therefore, the opportunity for family members to live together in a single household.

It was not until later that the noneconomic meaning of migration became clear. Changes in child rearing patterns, in spouse relations, in the quality of affective relations, and ultimately in family size took generations to occur. It can be speculated that not only were affective needs more poorly met as the industrial period gained strength, but also that they became more important for effective functioning in the increasingly bureaucratized economy. Modern bureaucracies employ a large number of specialists with differing vocabularies and interests. These specialists are combined in differing ways to cope with changing problems. In this context it is extremely important that the interpersonal climate facilitates communication, coordination, and, therefore, effectiveness. Indeed, two contemporary analysts have concluded that "the growth of this necessarily more complex and sophisticated...communication network is fostered by an interpersonal style that emphasizes building strong relationships rather than just accomplishing the task per se."[23] In this context, then, one would expect the rapid development of institutions that will provide the "affective supports" necessary to develop adult skills in "building strong interpersonal relationships." In short, the industrial dilemma is one of developing institutions alternative to the traditional family that will meet affective needs.

7

Bureaucracy and the Educational Crisis

AMONG THE MAJOR social institutions of the United States, probably none has been criticized as consistently and severely as the school. Whatever their politics or interests, virtually all Americans believe that there is something seriously wrong with schooling. We shall examine several aspects of this crisis in schooling by referring to a selected group of writers who typify a variety of viewpoints among educational experts. Our purpose in reviewing different perspectives on education is to link educational realities with bureaucracy on the one hand, and with the prerequisites of personal development on the other.

The models of the school outlined in chapter 5 emphasized that corporation and factory school systems share two things in common: a bureaucratic organization and an emphasis on productivity. The family type school, on the other hand, like the traditional family, stresses affective support. The family school is one in which the student is able to gain knowledge of personal rather than social importance by exposure to a large range of experiences. The school structure, and especially teachers, provide the student with emotional support through acceptance of the idea that the best learning takes place through living, through the exploration of new social and technical relationships by the student. This emphasis on integrating the student into a wide range of relationships is to be contrasted with the bureaucratic values of hierarchy, complexity, and specialization found in the factory school. We found that in industrialized societies, the family school is the one most apt to create the preconditions for personal development. A school that is "actualizing" is one that not only inculcates certain basic skills but also provides love, affection, and esteem. In this chapter we explore two basic questions about contemporary education: (1) which of the educational models is most descriptive of contemporary education? and (2) what are the attitudes of educational writers about them, with particular reference to the role of bureaucratic values?

WHAT ARE SCHOOLS LIKE?*

According to Heath, schooling is characterized by student passivity, conformity, and value instability. He calls attention to a "historic transition" in the kinds of institutional power that affect young people:

> The family, church, and neighborhood are rapidly losing *their* power to nurture emotional spontaneity, rootedness, cooperative, intimate, and caring attitudes and skills, and stable integrative values. The mass media, peer culture, and the school which increasingly dominate the lives of young people, induce passivity and inhibition, conformity, and impersonalization, and conflicting and unstable values.[1]

These tendencies are most evident in larger schools. The evidence suggests that there is an inverse relation between

---

*The authors are indebted to Robert Friedman for the ideas and material in this section.

school size and humanistic climate; that is, "the larger the school, particularly schools of more than five hundred students, the more impersonal and bureaucratic its atmosphere."[2]

What is the origin and function of the passivity, conformity, and alienation noted above? We know, of course, that bureaucratic values such as subordination and impersonality intensify with increasing size; that is, larger structures tend to be more bureaucratic than smaller ones, including schools. But describing these bureaucratic values does not explain their origin and function.

According to Katz, schools are "imperial institutions designed to civilize the natives." Their main purpose is "to reflect and confirm the social structure that erected them," to attend to the inculcation of "dominant social and industrial values" through the mechanism of bureaucracy. The result is "school systems that treat children as units to be processed into particular shapes and dropped into slots roughly congruent with the status of their parents."[3]

The basic bureaucratic structure of American education was fixed by about 1880 and has not really changed much since that time.[4] That particular structure was not inevitable. It remains intact today simply because organizational possibilities other than bureaucracy were rejected. The bureaucratic mode of school organization prevailed because it was consistent with "bourgeois social attitudes." Through bureaucracy, "the myth of equal opportunities has been fostered, while the amount of social mobility has been strictly regulated."[5] A century ago, Katz says, certain relationships among bureaucracy, class bias, and racism emerged and remain fixed today. Change in one element requires concurrent change in the others if educational progress is to occur.

During the first half of the nineteenth century, Katz notes, four major models of educational organization operated: paternalistic voluntarism, democratic localism, corporate voluntarism, and incipient bureaucracy. At that time organizational controversies were largely over questions of school size, control, professionalism, and finance. During this period,

> the importance of organization derived from its mediating position between social structure and social change. Paternalistic voluntarism was the form of organization characteristic of education in the pre-industrial, mercantile city. Corporate voluntarism and democratic localism characterized rural areas and were proposed for urban places precisely at times of transition between mercantile and industrial stages of development. Incipient bureaucracy spread with incipient industrialization.[6]

Historically, the bureaucratic model of education featured and explicitly promoted structural centralization (e.g., one central board of education replacing the autonomy of sectional and township governing bodies), close supervision (such as could be achieved through full-time superintendents), professional expertise (demonstrated through proper credentials), and punctuality (reflecting industrial values). The diffusion of bureaucratic values was undeniable. Educational writers everywhere tended to compare education with industry.

> They often described their school systems as factories and used metaphors based on the corporation and the machine. Modern industry, they could see, had developed its remarkable capacity through a rational organization that stressed hierarchy, the division of labor, and intensive professional supervision. If those methods worked in industries as diverse as textiles and railroads, why would they not work in education?[7]

The industrial model of education had the important effect of creating a marketplace of opportunity for professionals with psychological training. At a crucial historical point, when the institutional structure of professional education was still in inchoate form, psychologists pursued career opportunities and built their professional structure in substantial part by focusing on the difficulties of goal achievement besetting educators.

Hall, Baldwin, Cattell, Whitmer, Munsterberg, Jastrow, Angell, to mention only the earliest, publicized the utility of psychological skills for solving technical problems associated with implementation of the bureaucratic approach. Moreover, the collective efforts of this group and some of their first students resulted in the staking out of a wide jurisdictional territory of subject matter and method that later became the basis for diverse groupings within the profession. Not by design, the end result was a large net of psychological ideas, concepts, and skills that linked education with industrial values.

The significance of the entry of psychologists into education lay in the fact that their technologies spoke to the social control and adaptation of individuals to the system. They did not focus upon institutional change. As a professional group, they attacked the manifestations of social problems within education, but they were conspicuous in their lack of involvement with the larger social controversies and reform movements of the period between 1890 and 1920. The social histories written about this period are striking in what they do not report about educational psychologists. The structure and ideology were clearly noncontroversial. Indeed, this is understandable since psychologists were cultivating the more conservative sector of business and industry.

In summary, psychologists were able to infuse their technologies within the institutional structure of diverse organizations that emerged by 1930. They were able to achieve important positions and influence within the top level of education's social structure. Their influence extended to formal and ancillary organizations such as graduate schools, professional societies, important nonprofit research and service organizations, and governmental bodies. Most of the specialized functional roles incorporated within lower schools were, or have come to be, dependent upon some constellation of psychological knowledge and techniques. Despite this diffusion, educational psychology has been able to maintain a fair degree of control over the use of its technologies. This has been accomplished by agreements among the professional associations at the national level that have been translated at the state level into legislative enactments. At crucial junctures, formal inter-professional committees have worked out guidelines pertaining to training and ethical usage. The patterning of careers and the socialization of educators to norms of usage and outlook have maintained a dominant psychological ethos in the professional culture of education.

Arthur Stinchcombe nicely summarizes the consequences of such events in explaining why organizations exhibit persistent historical social structures.

> But to mold careers, to allow outside organizations permanent control over some aspects of policy...is not only to mobilize social forces for present purposes. It is also to infuse the resulting structure with value, to make it an "institution" rather than a technical device.[8]

Since the inception of the bureaucratic school, every generation has produced educational critics who lament its structural rigidity, negative influence on student creativity and personality, poor capacity to transmit basic skills, poor emotional reinforcement, anti-individuality, and especially exploitation of poor children. Yet it is not surprising that the model is as alive as ever. The basic professional and allied economic and social forces that created the institutional patterns in the late 1800s are with us today. No alternative has been formulated despite nearly a century of criticism, says Katz.[9] Indeed, most innovations proposed in the twentieth century—ability grouping, the junior high school, guidance—are really extensions of psychological technology that reinforce the old bureaucratic model. It is no wonder then that some writers see the only hope for education as "deschooling."

THE HUMAN CONSEQUENCES OF
BUREAUCRATIC ADAPTATION

For Ivan Illich, all contemporary societies, whether capitalist or socialist, organize their schools in such a way as to reproduce their particular established order. But that effort is now failing. "We are witnessing," he says, "the end of the age of schooling."[10]

During the first half of this century, schools propagated an "egalitarian myth" contradicted by the "stratified society which its certificates produce." The current collapse of schools "is a sign of disaffection with the industrial mode of production." Schools have lost legitimacy as a means of determining competence and as a personal measure of social value. Schools pretend to serve as agents of equality but actually are devoted to the task of reproducing, not improving, the particular society in which they are found.[11] Industrial and educational values are no longer congruent, a point of view distinguishing Illich from other observers.

Schools, in addition to providing skilled labor for industry, are bureaucratic institutions that produce well-disciplined, obedient consumers. But these same consumers are dissatisfied with themselves and society.

> Schools have alienated man from his learning. He does not enjoy going to school: if he is poor, he does not get the reputed benefits; if he does all that is asked of him, he finds his security constantly threatened by more recent graduates; if he is sensitive, he feels deep conflicts between what is and what is supposed to be. He does not trust his own judgment and even if he resents the judgment of the educator, he is condemned to accept it and to believe himself that he cannot change reality.[12]

A sizeable number of writers relate the responses of students to their class in a way that has some interesting bearings on the diffusion of bureaucratic values into schooling. "Class" is a complex term, and not all writers who employ it mean quite the same thing. The two predominant uses in the material that follows are (1) social class, or persons of the same social level of prestige and esteem who consider themselves social equals, and (2) economic class, or persons who share similar material and power positions in society, especially income level and workplace position. While the two meanings are often confused, the first is typically employed by liberals, the second by socialists. Research predominantly reflecting the social-class perspective has produced several broad characterizations of schooling.

Schools have institutionalized the advantages of middle-class children over those from a lower-class background through class discrimination. Such discrimination shows up, it is charged, in preference for and reward of middle-class students who share their teacher's class background.

Assuming that the middle-class way of life is the appropriate model, and also assuming that the poor motivation of lower-class children must be explained independently of what happens in school, it is claimed that schools are not responsible for lower-class academic failures and weaknesses. But even if they are, not more than one in four lower-class students can be expected to absorb enough motivation and skill to become upwardly mobile because the educational system is overwhelmingly geared to middle-class values and orientations. To say that a school is middle class is to say some ominous things about students from lower-class backgrounds. They will suffer because it is not likely that schools will attend to their particular needs for nurturance. Can we accept a decision by schools that ignores a type of education geared to lower-class problems and life styles? The implications, says Corwin, are very serious.

> If the lower-class way of life is granted validity and if the schools are expected to be of relevance to lower-class motives and environment, then schools are failing as democratic institu-

tions. They have been neither relevant nor challenging to most lower-class youths, against whom they have discriminated in terms of curriculum, grades, facilities, quality of the teaching staff, teacher-pupil ratio, and in other ways. It is a paradox that a less bureaucratic segregated system for the lower class, independently financed and autonomous of the central school system, and responsible only to the lower class, may in the long run prove to be more egalitarian. Only in a specialized system can the missionary problems of motivating lower-class children for mobility and the more pressing problem of assisting the nonmobile more effectively to cope with their environment be considered simultaneously. Again, the solution, like the problem itself, is largely an organizational one.[13]

Corwin is to be commended for expressing concern over the disabilities inflicted by schools on lower-class children. But he might be faulted on the ground advanced by some school critics that the problem is political rather than organizational. From this perspective Corwin begs the central question: No matter how autonomous from the central school system, should educational programs for the poor be so different as to disadvantage its children from achieving success and status? On this matter we come back to basic questions. What is education for? How should its goals be implemented? And above all, what values should education serve? Corwin's emphasis on organizational change seems to ignore the transformation of the school into an agent of bureaucratic diffusion of industrial values that displace affective needs formerly served by schools.

Some writers who note the hierarchical nature of education and its class bias go the full distance of socialist analysis of schooling in a liberal-capitalist society. In the writings of Bowles and Gintis, and in those of Carnoy, for example, the emphasis is less on middle-class attitudes or cultural norms and more on the direct, coercive control of education at all levels by an economic ruling class. That process of control, according to this analysis, reflects no real interest in emotional nurturance or need satisfaction of the individual student but rather aims at producing a working or technical class capable and willing to service ruling-class interests. Those interests are partly expressed in the form of bureaucratic goal setting and processing of students.

The most recent and comprehensive analysis of American education from a socialist point of view is Samuel Bowles and Herbert Gintis's book, *Schooling in Capitalist America.*[14] Their major thesis is that the American educational system mirrors and helps reproduce the unequal class structure of the capitalist system. Education does not provide equality of opportunity for human development or for economic reward because under capitalism, education seeks to "reproduce the social relations of production." For this reason, "the imperatives of profit, not human capacities and technical realities...render U.S. schooling what it is."[15] Increasingly, the social structure and processes of the school resemble those of the workplace. Through that resemblance, "the educational system reproduces the capitalist social division of labor."[16] Education neither increases nor decreases the amount of inequality in a capitalist society. Rather, its primary function is to facilitate the smooth integration of youth into the labor force. If the bureaucratic structure of the workplace is alienating, so is that found in education.

> Major aspects of the structure of schooling can be understood in terms of the systemic needs for producing reserve armies of skilled labor, legitimating the technocratic-meritocratic perspective, reinforcing the fragmentation of groups of workers into stratified status groups, and accustoming youth to the social relationships of dominance and subordinancy in the economic system.[17]

Education helps reproduce capitalist social relations by promoting the requisite type of consciousness. That consciousness is produced in part through the process of bureaucratic diffusion we discussed earlier. Workplace emphasis on bureaucratic and technological values such as punctuality, specialization, and hierarchy have their counterparts in the educational structure and curriculum. Lack of control over their work environment means that workers and students do not possess "sufficient autonomy to express their creative needs and capacities."[18]

Beginning with the same general assumptions about American society, Carnoy provides more detail as to the consequences of an education that is governed by the ruling class. Unlike liberal writers, who tend to believe that everyone has an equal chance to be rewarded through hard work at school, Carnoy sees something quite different happening. He believes that the real purpose of formal schooling is not to disseminate knowledge or enable people to improve their income and status, but rather to serve "as an allocator of social roles, and only secondarily as a transmitter of cognitive knowledge."[19]

> Schools help maintain a hierarchical structure, and help ensure that the same class of people end up at the top of the hierarchy in each generation, and the same class at the bottom. We contend that schools are able to legitimize grossly unequal access to goods and services in a capitalist society by colonizing children and their families to believe in the brand of "meritocracy" implemented by the schools: the school system ostensibly grades individuals not according to family background, but according to cognitive ability. Yet, as we have argued, cognitive ability is highly correlated with an individual's social class, and both social class and the amount of schooling an individual gets are better explainers of future income than cognitive ability....
>
> In a pyramidal, capitalist hierarchy, *learning* in public schools is organized to maintain that hierarchical structure. Children do not learn about their environment from the perspective of their own reality, but from the white, wealthy view. Thus, poverty, drug addiction, and crime are an individual failing rather than the result of an inequitable and racist economy; technological progress is defined as sending a man to the moon rather than organizing a community medical clinic; and children are taught to compete for the limited

number of "top" positions in the society rather than working together to improve their collective condition. Thus, all children in school learn to evaluate society on grounds favorable to the rich and powerful.[20]

Success or failure in school is not an individual matter independent of one's class background. The class structure of capitalist economic institutions is reflected in a system of education through which one class "civilizes" another to ensure that social stability and elite control are maintained. A vital function of education is convincing students that their economic and social positions should be accepted. The specific content of the values diffused will vary according to one's place in the class structure and with workplace structure. For some, schooling is an experience in obedience, while for others it may be quite different. In the end, however, education serves the purposes of hierarchical values.

> Thus, we reach the conclusion that, for a relatively small group, capitalism and schooling serve individual needs and allow a wide range of choice in the type of work and life the individual pursues. Those in this small group feel a genuine sense of self-fulfillment and accomplishment, they like the kind of work they do, and they have the security of social position and accumulated wealth. But for the large majority, schooling in a hierarchical society is required to *limit* individual choice by *defining* well-specified and uncreative roles in the social and economic hierarchy. Schooling defines people's potential for them on the basis of the hierarchy's needs, not their own. Schooling for a hierarchical structure is therefore a colonizing device which sometimes changes the *kind* of choices people have, but still serves to limit control over their own lives.[21]

The foregoing survey of writings on the educational crisis identifies bureaucracy as one major impediment to need satisfaction and emotional nurturance in the school. Students are alienated in part because the school confronts them with bureaucratic experiences of impersonality, subordination, and specialization. Let us look somewhat more closely at some interconnections among school, bureaucracy, and alienation.

BUREAUCRACY AND ALIENATION

Veblen, one of the best and earliest students of bureaucracy, reacted very critically to the application of business standards of efficiency to collegiate education. He condemned the credit and grade-point systems as counterparts of the price system employed by business to reduce administrative problems to standardized, quantifiable units.[22] More recently, Blau has described the detrimental effect of such bureaucratic standards on the student's academic performance.[23]

A study by Anderson sought to provide "a more satisfactory test of the relationship between organizational bureaucratization and alienation from school by attempting to account for variance in the alienation scores of students in terms of the degree of bureaucratization found in their schools."[24] After collecting data from eighteen secondary schools in Ontario, Canada, during 1968-1969, the author concluded that bureaucratic structure "does account for a large proportion of the variance in alienation attributable to differences between schools."[25] These findings led the author to speculate that "less bureaucratic modes of school organization may produce higher levels of pupil achievement." This is a tempting hypothesis since students of low socioeconomic status (whose grades are often low) seem to attend more highly bureaucratized schools than do students of high status. This raises the interesting possibili'y that "the poor achievement of these pupils in school may be due partially to the way the schools are run, and not just to deficiencies in their background as much current literature would suggest."[26] Anderson found that the presence of bureaucratic characteristics appears to be strongly correlated with increasing alienation. Whether high achievement is evidence of self-actualization or successful bureaucratization remains, however, an interesting and open question.

SUMMARY

This survey of literature on schools points to a variety of basic criticisms and conclusions, including the following: Students are highly conformist. The school is increasing its influence over students while that of the family declines. Schools are very powerful in shaping attitudes that maintain the social and political status quo. They are conservative institutions devoted to perpetuating class inequalities and to training students for roles that will uphold an exploitive system of stratification. Middle-class values are carefully disseminated through the schools' formal and informal curricula. This is done at the expense of lower-class children and culture, which are delegitimized in both subtle and blatant ways. A "hidden curriculum" teaches children to accept certain social myths as reality, in particular the virtues of product consumption and gratification of material wants.

The idea that education can serve as the chief liberating force for the individual is an ideal that has had strong adherents throughout history. At the center of that ideal is the assumption that there is in each child a possibility for growth. A key method of unleashing potential is to provide the child with participatory experiences on the assumption that schools should treat all students as equals.

Unfortunately, many schools have come to define equality as standardization rather than freedom, as sameness rather than variety. In short, many schools have bureaucratized in the name of equality rather than individualized in the name of liberty. This has produced two results of great concern to parents and educators: weakness in transmitting basic skills to students, and school structures that do not permit individuals to grow and fulfill their capabilities.

Schools have shown concern for personality, to be sure, but not the type that places self-development ahead of institutional needs and standards.

The only type of personality the school can support and approve is one that fits smoothly into the institutional organization. This means that for the school to survive it can nurture and develop only those behaviors which do not conflict with its institutional needs. The extension of compulsory education laws and the increased amount of time, both in terms of hours each day and in added years, has brought a greater part of the population under institutional controls. If the schools, because of their structure, nurture only one type of personality, this would mean the development of one dominant life style. Of course, in terms of the well-functioning society no objection to this condition need be raised. The type of personality needed in the school is the same as that needed in the corporation.[27]

We concluded earlier that the cost of meeting needs in bureaucratic organizations is often an inability to meet the needs of love, esteem, and development, coupled with a general fear of change and innovation. In a welter of conflicting viewpoints, one element of substantial agreement does stand out in the literature on schooling: bureaucratic values have been powerfully diffused into and through the schools, however one might evaluate the consequences of that diffusion. No school critic has yet produced research demonstrating that bureaucratic organization is consistent with the achievement of actualizing experiences. Almost without exception, educational research identifies bureaucracy and the diffusion of bureaucratic values as a major factor in the contemporary educational crisis.

8

Political Power, Culture, and Participation

THE DISCUSSION OF model political communities in chapter 5 led to observations worth summarizing. We noted a distinction between democratic and elitist political systems. Whether one or the other system is preferable depends on the particular problem or goal in question, but the democratic type is superior where the meeting of personal needs is paramount and where no *a priori* judgments are made that the satisfaction of one person's needs should be given priority over another's. Personal development is enhanced by political systems that are participative. The democratic model links political experiences with broader social experiences and opportunities.

Social institutions encourage development to the extent that they are "open" to personal influence. The pattern of social institutions constitutes a definable type of political culture. A variety of such cultures are possible, and all have important implications for the extent to which participative politics is experienced.

Political systems enhance or frustrate the satisfaction of personal needs partly as a consequence of the type of political culture in which such systems are found. A political culture that puts the ordinary person in the mainstream of public policy-making is called a "civic culture." Taken literally, the civic culture concept is utopian since no existing system is known to approximate all the elements postulated. Yet some systems come closer than others to realizing the ideal elements; to that extent they are said to possess the minimal elements of the civic culture.

Significant levels of participation presuppose the dispersion and availability of power to the citizenry. In this sense, political culture is closely linked to power. When we ask "What are the facts about participation?" we must also address the related issues of the distribution of political power and the content of political culture.

POWER IN POLITICAL COMMUNITIES

The publication in 1956 of C. Wright Mills's *The Power Elite*[1] occasioned a torrent of scholarly and popular responses both in praise and criticism of his arguments. This book, taken together with Floyd Hunter's *Community Power Structure* of 1953, constitutes an important juncture in the efforts of social scientists to show how power is exercised in American politics and by whom. We shall subject these significant power studies to a brief examination, indicate some major criticisms of each, and then suggest how these studies relate to the problem of political participation.

The Power Elite

Mills begins his analysis of power in America by examining those institutions that exercise power in the most crucial areas of public policy. He identifies those institutions and the sorts of people who are in command. Finally, he attempts to demonstrate that those in command are interlocked and, because they share the same goals and values, actually "run" American society.

Presently, says Mills, major national power is found in the highest reaches of the economic, political, and military domains; other institutions are of comparatively minor importance. This means that the big three institutions increasingly shape such minor institutions as the school and the family. But what, more specifically, is "the power elite"?

> At the pinnacle of each of the three enlarged and centralized domains, there have arisen those higher circles which make up the economic, the political, and the military elites. At the top of the economy, among the corporate rich, there are the chief executives; at the top of the political order, the members of the political directorate; at the top of the military establishment, the elite of soldier-statesmen clustered in and around the Joint Chiefs of Staff and the upper echelon. As each of these domains has coincided with the others, as decisions tend to become total in their consequences, the leading men in each of the three domains of power — the warlords, the corporation chieftains, the political directorate — tend to come together, to form the power elite of America.[2]

This elite also includes "men of the higher legal and financial type from the great law factories and investment firms, who are almost professional go-betweens of economic, political and military affairs, and who thus act to unify the power elite."[3] The interlocking character of this elite is found in the fact that members (1) share the same basic interests (such as military expenditures); (2) interchange control of commanding roles at the top of the various institutions; (3) possess common origins, background, and educational experiences that lead to rather similar psychological orientations; and (4) associate intimately with one another in their social and business lives. As Mills sums it up: "They accept one another, understand one another, marry one another, tend to work and to think if not together at least alike."[4]

Congress represents the "middle reaches" of power and is therefore subordinate to the power elite. Decisions about war and peace and about economic decline or prosperity, in short the "big" questions, are made by the power elite. All other decisions tend to be made at the Congressional level, which reflects the particular interests of interest groups of all sorts (farmers, union members, business and so on). At this middle level, special pleading, bargaining, competition, and compromise take place. It is a pluralistic world in which almost everyone gets into the act.

Below the middle level of power lies "mass society," the vast citizenry that receives more opinions than it expresses, that finds it increasingly difficult to react to government, that realizes that the mass media are strictly controlled in terms of access and content, and that politics is increasingly controlled by formal institutions that reduce personal freedom and expression. The extent to which America has become a mass society is an index to the increasing power of the controlling elite at the top.

> At the top there has emerged an elite of power. The middle levels are a drifting set of stalemated, balancing forces: the middle does not link the bottom with the top. The bottom of this society is politically fragmented, and even as a passive fact, increasingly powerless. At the bottom there is emerging a mass society.[5]

The critical reactions to Mills's idea of the power elite were not long in coming — and they came from all over the political spectrum. Here we can only deal briefly with several of the critical responses, focusing on those most relevant to the topic of political participation.

Is the power elite in fact a cohesive group? Is there "a fair sample of cases involving key political decisions in which the preferences of the hypothetical ruling elite run counter to those of any other likely group that might be suggested?" Do the preferences of the elite usually prevail? Robert Dahl raised these questions in a thoughtful critique of Mills, answering no to all of them.[6]

As we have noted, the principal segments of Mills's power elite encompass elements of three main social institutions: the corporate, military, and political worlds. He was criticized by some scholars for exaggerating the power of business, while others criticized him for understating that power.[7] A number of Mills's supporters rejected his assertion that a military clique plays an independent political role as part of the elite, arguing that the American military has traditionally been nonpolitical and subordinate to political leadership. Regarding the political segment of the power elite, Mills's critics argued that he underestimated the power roles of Congress, political parties, and interest groups, and also that he failed to appreciate the great pressures brought to bear on those in high places, pressures that often succeeded. Another criticism in this context was that the President, not an elite, makes war and peace decisions such as military intervention or the use of atomic weapons.

A final objection to *The Power Elite* concerned the mass society thesis of the increasing impotence or absence of popular opinion in decision making. "The proletariat," said Mills, "doesn't make history, no matter how much you want to stretch historical facts."[8] This was a direct slap at Marxists, who believe in the political role of the working class, and a criticism of liberals, who believe that the masses control a democracy.

Pluralist Democracy

Partly in response to *The Power Elite*, Dahl published *Who Governs?*,[9] a study of political power and participation in New Haven, Connecticut. From this work and others, there emerged a general political theory of democracy called pluralism, an explanation of how and why political power in the United States is dispersed rather than centralized.[10] The conclusions Dahl reached, as we shall see, almost wholly contradict those reached by Mills.

Dahl decided to study key decisions in which power is exercised rather than studying reputations for being powerful. This method made "an attempt...to study specific outcomes, in order to determine who actually prevails in community decision-making."[11] Among the many possible key decisions that could be studied, several were picked because they got to the heart of the question as to whether New Haven was democratic. After careful consideration, the following areas were selected because "key political decisions" were made in each, decisions involving the life of the entire community: public education, urban renewal, and party nominations. Dahl assumed, like Mills, that only a few persons actually make important decisions, but what he wanted to know was the extent or scope of power exercised by those few people. If (as he discovered) he could determine that the scope of power was limited and that decision makers were responsible to the people below, he would have demonstrated that democracy in New Haven was alive and well. Dahl did, finally, discover a political elite, but it was not the highest social and economic group of the city. He also discovered that public power in one area of decision making did not necessarily extend to others. Dahl determined that political power in New Haven was not cumulative, in contrast to Mills who claimed that it was. In Dahl's view, power is a set of resources, such as money, credit, jobs, expertise, influence, and social position. Dahl found that the resources comprising political power are noncumulative, therefore no small group had irresistible power in community affairs. The upshot of the noncumulative character of power resources is that while they are unevenly distributed, no one has a monopoly on them; conversely, every person had access to some set of resources that could change the political landscape some of the time.

Dahl found that the political stratum of the city is an open circle that anyone can join, whatever one's interests or group affiliation. "The independence, penetrability, and heterogeneity of the various segments of the political stratum all but guarantee that any dissatisfied group will find spokesmen in the political stratum."[12] In short, significant participatory opportunities are ensured because everyone can become a part of the pluralistic political decision-making process.

Apoliticals are those who have resources but do not use them ordinarily. Such resources constitute "slack" or potential power that can be brought to bear effectively against any political leaders who violate their trust and refuse to satisfy the needs of the public. Hence, those in the apolitical stratum have available a resource called indirect influence, a resource sufficiently potent to persuade politicians to anticipate and satisfy the needs of that large segment of the citizenry.

Critics faulted the pluralistic theory of Dahl and his associates on several grounds. Some critics complained about the specific issues chosen for analysis on the ground that only observable conflict was taken into consideration, while other forms of conflict not on public political agenda were ignored. Indeed, some critics noted that elite power may be so great as to prevent any open conflict or disagreement from being expressed.[13] This criticism was often linked to the observation that Dahl chose to analyze public power and decisions while ignoring the enormous amount of private power that influences public decision making and the welfare of all citizens.

The power to exclude matters from public discussion is called "nondecision making." That is, some people decide that certain matters will not be discussed, acted on, or even considered. The decision not to legitimize certain issues results from a "mobilization of bias" process. In any community, the scope of actual decision making is usually limited to "safe" issues that will maintain the status quo and, therefore, the interests, myths, rituals, institutions, and so forth of the community's dominant groups. On certain matters this bias may be powerful enough to foreclose any consideration or action, as in the case of race relations after the Civil War.

AN HISTORICAL PERSPECTIVE

Greater sense can be made of these conflicting theories of community power if they are taken in historical perspective. Robert O. Schulze properly notes that "Relatively little research attention has yet been devoted to historical shifts in local power structures associated with metropolitan and bureaucratic drift of American life."[14] The inconsistency in the community power findings may be due in part to the fact that communities differ in their level of economic development. While all communities are generally experiencing industrialization and bureaucratization, there are leading and lagging communities. A feature of industrialization not emphasized to this point but that seems central to political power and participation is the extent to which local economies are integrated into regional, national, and international economic structures. Schulze hypothesizes that

> in the community relatively self-contained and uninvolved in the larger social and economic system, the community with few and scattered commitments beyond its borders, local power would tend to be structured as a pyramid and heavily concentrated at the apex. With increasing urbanization and... "the period of local capitalism" the economic dominants would begin to withdraw their interest and active attention from the local socio-political system.[15]

The basic logic of Schulze's withdrawal argument is that because the local community eventually becomes less important to the prosperity of its dominant economic units, there is less incentive for the influential to become actively involved in local politics. The political and social aspects of community life might be controlled by one set of elites, but the local economic system might be controlled by another whose roots and interests are largely outside the community.

In order to test this notion, Schulze studied the economic dominants in a small midwestern city from agricultural through postindustrial periods (1823-1955). He found that prior to the turn of the century, 70 percent of the town's economic dominants held public office, while after 1900 the proportion dropped to 25 percent. Indeed, not a single manager of a large corporation operating in the town held public office since the turn of the century.

> Our research established that in the pre-1900 period, almost 70 percent of the economic dominants had known business or financial ties—as partners, co-officers or co-directors—with other dominants in the community. Thus, throughout Cibola's history, its "average" economic dominant was not only a local resident, or merely the head of a single major economic unit; he was also directly and indirectly linked with a considerable number of other major economic units and dominants within the community.[16]

The picture has changed dramatically since 1900 because of the establishment of local industrial units that have direct ties to large nonlocal manufacturing enterprises, the growth of branch plants of large absentee-owned corporations, and the dissolution of extensive networks of interlocking directorships and officerships "which had formerly served to link significant numbers of local economic dominants with the community."[17] The consequence of a lack of interest in local political matters by economic dominants was that influence over political matters passed largely to professionals and small business people who were not part of the economic elite.

While not conclusive, this research supports the idea that there are facets of community life that extend to matters not directly concerned with affairs of crucial interest to economic dominants. Increasingly, the latter's interests are tied to higher governments, larger markets, or national and international corporate structures. Lack of interest in local politics by officers of outside businesses and corporations may be due to the mobility of corporate life and the lack of family roots in the community, as well as to product demands being generated nationally through the media and to supply factors being part of national and international markets.

The withdrawal of economic dominants from local politics is crucial for questions of political power and participation because it is a major element in the increasingly pluralistic structure of community power. Reflecting on the transformations in New Haven politics, Robert Dahl notes that

> these [changes]...reflected profound alterations in the community, in the course of which important resources for obtaining influence were fragmented and dispersed. Wealth was separated from social position by the rise of industry, and public office went to the wealthy. Later, popularity was divorced from both wealth and social position by the influx of immigrants, and public office went to the ex-plebes, who lacked wealth and social position but had the advantage of numbers.[18]

In the preindustrial period, then, power tended to be concentrated in communities because the resources for power and meaningful participation were concentrated. Wealth, social position, and popularity were combined in the hands of a relatively small group of local leaders. In the industrial and postindustrial periods, the resources for power became more dispersed and therefore the pattern of power and participation more pluralistic. But only in a sense. That is, many basic issues simply disappeared from the public agenda, their place often taken by secondary matters. Local political communities have become more pluralistic and less important at the same time. It appears that more major decisions are being made at the national and international levels.

A recent look at some of these issues is taken by Thomas Dye in *Who's Running America?*[19] Dye's analysis begins with the observation that the nation's resources are concentrated in a relatively small number of large institutions, an observation we made earlier in the context of industrial development.

> Half of the nation's industrial assets are concentrated in 100 manufacturing corporations; half of the nation's banking assets

are concentrated in the 50 largest banks; half of the nation's assets in transportation, communications, and utilities are concentrated in 33 corporations; two-thirds of the nation's insurance assets are concentrated in just 18 companies; 12 foundations control nearly 40 percent of all foundation assets; 12 universities control 54 percent of all private endowment funds in higher education; 3 network broadcasting companies control 10 percent of the television news, and 10 newspaper chains account for one-third of the daily newspaper circulation. It is highly probable that 30 Wall Street and Washington law firms exercise comparable dominance in the legal field and that a dozen cultural and civic organizations dominate music, drama and arts, and civic affairs.[20]

Given the concentration of resources in large institutions, the nation's powerful, Dye reasons, will be those who control these large institutions. The extent of pluralism or hierarchy in the polity is indicated not only by the number of institutional elites but also by the extent to which they "interlock" with one another. That is, the case for a hierarchical polity is stronger if a relatively small number of people hold top positions in several of the largest institutions. Dye finds that "approximately four thousand individuals in five thousand positions exercise formal authority over institutions that control roughly half of the nation's resources in industry, finance, utilities, insurance, mass media, foundations, education, law and civic and cultural affairs."[21]

Dye also found that 80 percent of the institutional elites identified held only one of the top five thousand institutional positions, although they usually held many lesser positions in corporate, civic, and cultural organizations in addition to their top institutional position. Although there is substantial "specialization" of institutional elites,

> there are...important concentrations of combined corporate, governmental, and social power in America. These concentrations center about the great, wealthy, entrepreneurial families — the Rockefellers, Mellons, duPonts, Fords. Doubtlessly the

most important of these concentrations is in the Rockefeller family group, which has an extensive network in industrial, financial, political, civic, educational, and cultural institutions.[22]

Dye's work and that of others[23] probably establishes that a relatively small number of elites occupy the highest positions in institutions controlling the majority of resources important for political power. The outstanding issue, however, is the extent to which the people in these positions in fact directly control the resources of the institutions they formally head. Perhaps the best work on this question is provided by Arnold Tannenbaum's[24] study of industrial enterprises in five societies (United States, Austria, Italy, Yugoslavia and Israel). From the onset, there never seems to have been a serious question about the actual hierarchical distribution of control in the plants studied. For all countries, the higher the formal positions, the more likely the feeling that one exercises substantial control. It was also found, however, that the gradients of authority and reward that accompany hierarchy differ in magnitude between systems, with Italian, Austrian, and American plants being substantially more hierarchical than Israeli and Yugoslav plants.

Which of the competing theories about community power does the evidence corroborate? Probably neither. Many communities are becoming more pluralistic, more participative. But, one must ask, in relation to what kinds of political decisions? Our view is that the locus of power is rapidly changing from the local to the regional, national, and even international levels. There is much pluralism and participation at the local level, but not of a type that changes basic power in the community. Indeed — and this is ironic, to be sure — some communities have become more and more pluralistic about less and less.

The extent and type of political participation (from the simple act of voting through influence over important public decisions) is decisively influenced by the values, norms, and expectations of a particular community of people. Taken together, these elements may be said to comprise a political culture, which includes certain bureaucratic values that are a part of the larger general culture of the community. Political culture, then, defines possibilities, directions, and boundaries for the exercise of political participation. Let us look more closely at political culture as a determinant of citizen participation.

The Idea of Political Culture

"Every political system," says Gabriel A. Almond, "is embedded in a particular pattern of orientations to political action. I have found it useful to refer to this as the *political culture*."[25] Almond notes that political culture "is a differentiated part of the [general] culture and has a certain autonomy." The concept is especially useful in studying political participation because it emphasizes the psychological dimensions of a political system—the attitudes, beliefs, expectations, and symbols that individuals hold about their perceived chances to satisfy needs through involvement in the political process.

The political culture approach to participation is valuable because it refers to the individual's "system of empirical beliefs, expressive symbols, and values which defines the situation in which political action takes place."[26] Ultimately, how one feels about the extent or quality of one's political participation is a subjective matter. Hence, political culture "refers not to what is happening in the world of politics, but what people believe about these happenings."[27]

How and how much an individual wants to participate in politics depends on one's orientations to the political system. Orientation refers to the consciousness of political objects and their importance for the individual. Almond and Verba describe as parochials those persons who exhibit little or no awareness of the national political system. Among those who do manifest awareness, a distinction may be drawn between subjects and participants. Subjects are persons who are sensitized to the processes and consequences of the system but are not directly involved in it. Participants are those who are "oriented to the input [i.e., policy-making] structures and processes, and engage in, or view themselves as potentially engaging in, the articulation of demands and the making of decisions."[28] Political cultures may be classified according to the relative dominance of parochials, subjects, and participants.

Parochial political cultures, according to Almond and Verba, are those lacking specialized political roles, those in which little or no distinction exists among political, economic, and religious functions. Participation is not an issue at all, for the individual displays no specifically "political" orientation; indeed, the individual expects nothing at all from the political system. Hence the central government, and politics itself, remains an obscure and negative phenomenon to most persons.

Subject political cultures are characterized by political orientations, but these orientations are toward outputs rather than inputs; that is, toward awareness of governmental authority and policy enforcement but not toward feelings of participant competence and interest in effecting public policy. The individual remains in a passive relationship to government, not a participatory one.

Participant political cultures possess a citizenry oriented toward active involvement in the political system. While the particular feelings that accompany such involvement may be positive or negative, the basic orientation can be described as one of commitment to and active concern over political affairs.

No society completely embodies any of these categories, for partial manifestations of each probably exist in most political systems. With few exceptions, all political cultures are mixed, though in different proportions and with widely varying consequences. When a political culture remains mixed for a long period of time, "there are inevitable strains between culture and structure, and characteristic tendency toward structural instability."[29]

The "civic" culture, one of the mixed types, contains individuals who feel a strong involvement with political outputs as well as the processes that produce them. Hence, the civic culture "is a participant political culture in which the political culture and political structure are congruent."[30] Subject and parochial orientations complement participant orientations, leading to "a balanced political culture in which political activity, involvement, and rationality exist but are balanced by passivity, traditionality and commitment to parochial values."[31] According to Nie (see table 8.1) the United States and Britain are prototypes of the civic culture, though they differ considerably in various particulars. For example, the lower class in the United States, which in all cultures participates at low levels, is relatively small compared to other countries studied. It is generally true that citizens in the United States and the other industrialized countries are more likely to belong to organizations. The political significance of this is that organizational membership is associated with participant orientations. The group context of membership provides incentives for participation but also restrains extreme forms of political involvement. There is a high correlation between social class and organizational involvement in the United States compared to Britain, Germany, Italy, and Mexico. This is explained in part by the fact that the three European countries exerted considerable and successful efforts to create party and other organizational structures specifically for the lower class.

These findings are consistent with those of Almond and Powell that "a great deal of evidence exists to suggest that increase in educational level and socioeconomic status are closely related to level of political awareness, participation, and feeling of political competence."[32] The industrialized countries have a larger proportion of "participants" because material well-being, which tends to be produced by industrialization, also allows higher levels of education, a condition precedent to political awareness and sense of political involvement. These findings

TABLE 8.1.   SOCIAL STRUCTURE AND CLASS GROUP PARTICIPATION: FIVE NATIONS.

Nation	Class structure of society: Proportion in low, middle, upper classes			Organizational density: Proportion of citizens belonging to organizations	Class-organization correlation	Overall participation rate: Percent classified as politically active*
	L	M	U			
United States	30 percent	45 percent	25 percent	55 percent	.44	46
Britain	46	38	16	49	.31	45
Germany	44	41	15	39	.21	40
Italy	54	32	14	27	.30	27
Mexico	77	16	7	20	.23	25

*Being classified as "politically active" is roughly equivalent to discussing politics at least once a week, or more active involvement, as measured by scale items.

Source: Norman H. Nie, G. Bingham Powell, Jr., and Kenneth Prewitt, "Social Structure and Political Participation: Developmental Relationships, II," *American Political Science Review*, 63 (Sept. 1969), p. 824. Reprinted by permission.

are elaborated in Almond and Verba's study of five nations. They found:

1. Better education, membership in a majority ethnic or religious group, and higher socioeconomic status are clearly associated with feelings of political efficacy.
2. Educational differences more than any others explain varying levels of political confidence. That is, well-educated persons tend to feel more efficacious than less well-educated persons.

Political alienation is the other face of efficacy. Before turning to some recent data on this subject, let us indicate in more detail what alienation means.

Powerlessness refers to the feeling that one has lost personal efficacy, the ability to act influentially and significantly within the political arena. The powerless person feels unable to influence or control events within the immediate environment. In extreme form, powerlessness leads to a sense of futility or hopelessness about exerting control over those who "run things." Normlessness refers to the feeling that the standards or rules that constitute one's values and that govern one's behavior have been rejected as evidenced by widespread immoral conduct, especially on the part of political leaders. All this is experienced as the loss or disintegration of one's own standards. There is a strong feeling that governing values are imposed on the individual by others.

How much alienation of this sort is found in the public? Do Americans perceive great inequality in the disposition of political power? If they do, how much insistence is there on corrective measures such as popular political participation? Does the American public think that their system is elitist or democratic?

For answers and perspectives related to some of these questions, we turn to a comprehensive report on popular sentiments about American government prepared for the United States

Senate by the Louis Harris polling organization and published as a government document in 1973.[33] We shall hereafter refer to this as the CC Survey. The basic purpose of the study was to measure public perception of the responsiveness of government at all levels, and to explore ways to increase the responsiveness and efficiency of government. Two broad conclusions were reached in the study: (1) "The American people's loss of confidence in their government has reached severe — even majority — proportions today, but, at the same time, the American people overwhelmingly believe that government at all levels can be made to work effectively and well." Indeed, "the people — to a degree far greater than leaders understand — appear prepared to participate in the decisions that shape their society." (2) "A symptom of the distance between government and the governed is the distance between the opinions of the public and their leaders." The people and government officials disagree significantly on such matters as the quality of life, trust in news sources, whether or not there is something "deeply wrong" with American society, and whether or not more monitoring of public officials is needed, with the ordinary citizen generally more critical than officials. Two tables from that survey are reproduced here. We shall comment on a few of the findings as they link political alienation to certain aspects of political participation.

In table 8.2, the powerlessness dimension is represented by items 1, 3, 4, 5, 7, 11, 12. Normlessness is represented by items 6, 8, 9. In general, we find significant levels of powerlessness and normlessness in the "Total" percentages reported (first column). There is strong agreement that the gap between rich and poor is widening (76 percent), that tax laws benefit primarily the wealthy (74 percent), and that special interests are the chief beneficiaries of government (74 percent). Regarding the normlessness items, note that a majority of the respondents believe that most elective officials value self-benefit over public interest (60 percent), that government officials do not care

TABLE 8.2.   AGREEMENT WITH STATEMENTS OF ALIENATION.

	Total percent	Eighth Grade percent	High School percent	College percent
1. The rich get richer and the poor get poorer.	76	78	80	68
2. Wire-tapping and spying under the excuse of national security is a serious threat to people's privacy.	75	74	75	74
3. The tax laws are written to help the rich, not the average person.	74	78	75	69
4. Special interests get more from the government than the people do.	74	69	75	74
5. What you think doesn't count very much anymore.	61	68	64	54
6. Most elective officials are in politics for all they can get out of it for themselves.	60	70	64	51
7. The federal government in Washington has been trying to dictate too much what people locally can and cannot do.	59	58	64	53

145

(Table 8.2 continued)

8. The people running the country don't really care what happens to you.	55	57	51
9. Most people with power try to take advantage of people like yourself.	55	60	44
10. Local government is so disorganized, it's hard to know where to go for help.	49	49	44
11. You feel left out of things going on around you.	29	32	21
12. Important things that happen in the world don't affect your life.	22	22	18

From a report by Louis Harris polling organization prepared for the U.S. Senate and published as a government document in 1973.

about the individual (55 percent), and that most people with power try to exploit others.

The CC Survey also presents data on alienation and powerlessness between 1966 and 1973 (see table 8.3). Note that in every instance, the degree of alienation reported increases to a peak figure for 1973. These findings are reflected in the "Change" column showing positive percentage increases in agreement with the alienation statements on the left.

Nie et al. came to essentially the same conclusion in their study of American voting behavior between 1958 and 1972.[34] The voting patterns of the American electorate seemed to indicate that increased education had increased interest in politics, which "leads to increased attitude consistency (with the 1964 election as catalyst); increased consistency leads to growing dissatisfaction with the government and the parties (with the divisive issues of the late 1960s as catalyst)." Gelb and Palley[35] have taken these conclusions and tied them to the development of the postindustrial society.

The rise in education tends to coincide with the emergence of technologically intensive forms of production. Modern modes of production require the capacity to make relatively complicated decisions rather than physical labor. Decision making in turn requires sophistication in information processing. Specific aspects of sophistication are logical, mathematical, and language skills, all the product of education. Gelb and Palley argue that the "informational" sophistication characteristic of the postindustrial society has led to a deepened desire to effectively participate in political decisions.

The picture one gets of contemporary American politics is one in which the pattern of industrial development has made effective popular control more difficult, yet more desired. The postindustrial society is one in which power has become more national and international, while at the same time the mass citizenry is more educated and more aware of the need to have some influence over political outcomes. Perhaps the

TABLE 8.3.   TREND IN ALIENATION AND POWERLESSNESS FELT BY THE AMERICAN PEOPLE.

Agree with Statement	1973 percent	1972* percent	1971 percent	1968 percent	1966 percent	Change 1966-1973 percent
1. The rich get richer and the poor get poorer.	76	68	62	54	45	+31
2. What you think doesn't count much anymore.	61	53	44	42	37	+24
3. People running the country don't really care what happens to you.	55	50	41	36	26	+29
4. Feel left out of things going on around you.	29	25	20	12	9	+20
Average feeling alienated and powerless	55	49	42	36	29	+26

From a report by Louis Harris polling organization prepared for the U.S. Senate and published as a government document in 1973.

*These figures came from a survey conducted in May 1972 and do not reflect the one sharp drop in the overall "average feeling alienated and powerless" measurement that was recorded in a poll taken just before the November 1972 elections. That poll gave an overall alienation level of 41, but this departure from the steady upward trend of the 1966-1973 measurements was of extremely brief duration.

documented dissatisfaction with government and the party system is a reflection of these conflicting trends. The CC Survey concluded that the public believes that there is a new political crisis.

> The crisis the people addressed themselves to in this study is broad and deep. It involves the basic elements of trust and confidence in government. A precondition for responsiveness is a disposition on the part of the people to believe in their own influence on government. On this count, there is virtually no evidence that the American people are spoiling to change the basic structure of their free and voluntary society. To the contrary, if anything, the people opt for an even more pluralistic and responsibility-sharing system, involving more dialogue and more contact between leaders and led, as well as more division of the labor of governing among the federal, state, and local levels.
>
> Perhaps even more important, the people also want to see themselves and the citizens groups they feel could represent them have a much more important place in the governmental process. The public feels deeply that it can and would participate much more than now in a more open and inviting process.[36]

Does the American public regard the system as elitist or democratic? There is evidence to suggest that the system is perceived as elitist, and as hierarchical in terms of power distribution. How then has the public responded to its own perception? In theory, three answers are possible. First, the public may feel that upward mobility ("getting ahead" or achieving the "better life") is within everyone's reach provided they work hard, set high goals of achievement, pursue success vigorously, and learn the virtues of perseverance. In this context, political elitism would not be defined as a bar to self-improvement. A second possible response would indicate belief in the necessity of fundamental institutional changes, particularly in the economic and political spheres, which may be perceived as "bankrupt" or "failing." And third, the public could hold that the elitist character of society justifies withdrawal from politics on the ground that the organization of power is irrelevant to one's true interests and needs or, conversely, on the ground that "the system" is beyond saving through political action. The first response implies responsible citizenship and belief in improvement through faith in the system. The second may be described as the posture of political radicalism. The third option has been described through such vague terms as "apathy" and "retreatism."

We are unable to say with certainty which of these responses expresses "the" public mood. Short of a definitive statement, however, one can say with some confidence that most of the studies carried out in the last decade place primary emphasis on the first and third responses, that is, belief of the public in the possibility of upward mobility and apathy, but with the latter taking a stronger hold at the expense of the former in recent years. What kind of power reality does that response presuppose? It presupposes a view of political reality in which power is distributed unevenly and often used to "hurt" the "little people," but control of power by the "big boys" is neither an absolute deterrent to nor an excuse for denying the possibilities for self-improvement.

The CC Survey, cross-national studies, and voting studies provide evidence that reveal strong, extensive public feelings of powerlessness and suggest that the public feels "pushed around" or "out of it." On the other hand, the evidence also suggests a strong belief in the necessity and possibility of holding public officials accountable to moral norms of political conduct. Hence, the responses may be interpreted as a call for responsible elites monitored by public review of decision making. This interpretation suggests that some citizens regard political elitism and democratic participation as consistent and complementary rather than contradictory.

In chapter 5 we discussed two models of political community, the elitist and the participative. We believe that the participative model is more facilitative of personal development. For many people, perhaps most, a good political system must be one in which individuals are a part of the process through which public policy ends are set and met. It is simply not enough to have "responsible elites;" one must take part in the evolution of policy.

How does one account for public acceptance of the responsible elite theory of politics? Again, research does not permit a clear answer to this important question, but it is our view that it reflects the successful diffusion of bureaucratic values to the citizenry. That is, acceptance of elitist power may be partially accounted for by the role of bureaucratic power in society.

It was noted above that the public still tends to believe that it has the right to hold leaders accountable. Elites ought not have a free hand, although they are permitted great latitude. How do we account for the public taking this middle ground? A possible answer to this question relates to the interaction of the primary institutions. The major conclusions of the chapters on the family and the school were that schools are failing to provide substantive knowledge and analytical skills to their students, and that families are getting smaller but failing to provide basic affective support to children. Taken together, these trends imply a public that increasingly feels deprived but unable to act responsibly to reduce deprivation. Without adequate knowledge and analytic skills, people cannot realistically be expected to form a participatory public. Feelings of interpersonal deprivation do not disappear even with educational sophistication, and at the level of the individual cry out for amelioration. The strategy of responsible elites seems consistent with these conditions. The mass public, acutely aware of its problems but feeling incompetent to act in its own behalf, looks to those who presumably know how to get results, are technically competent, and are concerned with the public's problems.

9

The Emerging Loss of Trust and Legitimacy in Society

WE HAVE INDICATED that the capacity of individuals to develop depends on their power. Power is necessary because personal development requires a capacity to set goals that are consistent with one's interests, skills, and aspirations and to have control over the resources necessary for their attainment. It was also recognized that there are several aspects to understanding the process by which some persons come to possess a great deal of power while others have relatively little. The approach that seemed particularly appropriate to understanding bureaucratic power emphasizes the acceptance of bureaucratic values that historically have been part of the exchange processes between subordinates and superiors in organizations. The basis of bureaucratic power is willing acceptance of organizational values, even when they may not be entirely consistent with individual needs.

An historical analysis of bureaucratic values strongly suggested that the driving forces in their establishment are the requirements of industrial production. Relatedly, we suggested that the structure and underlying values of the family, school, and polity have been shaped and formed in response to these same industrial forces.

Industrialism has resulted in substantial material advancement, but the price has been widespread legitimization of the ideas of hierarchy and impersonality. In our judgment, these ideas have detracted from the ability of the family, school, and polity to perform as effectively as they might their core functions of meeting individual needs for affection and personal growth. Hierarchy and impersonality do not encourage personal growth, indeed may threaten such growth, principally because they serve interests other than those central to the individual. Impersonality, for example, may well be vital to the ongoing work of a bureaucratically organized public or private agency, but it is hardly appropriate for improving basic relations between children and parents. In this sense, the core functions of the family tend to become displaced by the diffusion of bureaucratic values whose origins and purposes are essentially alien to the ties that bind family members together.

In this final chapter we explore what seems to be a crisis for primary institutions but also, ironically, for large organizations. This is the crisis of legitimacy and trust in institutions, including bureaucratic ones. Our argument is simply that the emphasis on hierarchy and impersonality, successfully diffused to the primary institutions, has so severely damaged them that their efficacy in generating trust and legitimacy, including their capacity to legitimate bureaucratic values and trust in industrial organizations, has been severely weakened.

THE FAILURE OF POSTINDUSTRIALISM AND THE EMERGING INDUSTRIAL ORDER

That industrialism has reshaped the fabric of society is not disputed. There is, however, serious debate about whether some of the basic dynamics of this process are undergoing a fundamental transformation. Clark Kerr and his colleagues argue that the industrial system represents a set of forces that are becoming stronger.

> By the middle of the twenty-first century, industrialization will have swept away most preindustrial forms of society, except possibly for a few odd backwaters. This is the greatest transformation in the long history of mankind on this planet — more basic, more rapid, more universal than any other transformation.[1]

These are rather expansive claims. Kerr's arguments are buttressed by a description of the commitments of elites who are the leading forces for change in various countries. "Industrialism is introduced by either native or alien elites; by groups of men who seek to conquer the society through the superiority of the new means of production."[2] He suggests that while the idea of industrialism in eighteenth-century England was promoted by middle-class elites who glorified individual effort, the open market, and a certain amount of social conflict, the acceptance of industrialism spread to other elites with very different objectives and strategies. Today, dynastic elites see industrialization as a way to preserve traditional society and their paternal leadership of it. The worker remains dependent on the regime, and conflict is suppressed. Revolutionary elites rely on a highly centralized state that operates to force a rapid transformation.

Kerr argues that the common element that unifies these diverse elites in their commitment to industrialization is, literally, the prospect of oblivion.

> A military defense now requires a relatively advanced industrial technology. The military bases and operations of the great powers have demonstrated to the farthest corners of the globe...the invincibility of the giant of industrialization. Nonindustrial societies are ultimately destined to be consigned to the rear ranks of nations.[3]

Even the accumulation of great wealth will not slow the enthusiasm for industrialism. Pointed examples are the oil-rich nations of the Middle East. Saudi Arabia has among the largest cash reserves of any state in the world. Yet its very existence is threatened by the fact that it must import virtually all of its strategic resources, including military hardware and the very means of physical survival, food.

Industrial capacity is essential not only to protect a regime from external military threats but also to help assure internal political stability. S. M. Lipset and others have shown that stable economic growth is strongly associated with political stability. Failure of an economic system to keep pace with popular economic expectations commonly results in demands for political change. Economic and political elites thus have an enormous stake in the vitality and persistence of the industrial system. It is a necessary condition for the buffering of internal demands and for protection against the designs of those outside one's borders.

But who are the new elites in the most advanced industrial societies and what type of structures do they control? What are their prospects? These are important issues because, if our analysis is correct, their goals and values will become important shapers of bureaucratic values in the years ahead.

EMERGING BUREAUCRATIC STRUCTURES AND ELITES

Since the 1960s many writers concerned with the impact of bureaucracy on society have tended to forecast a rather idyllic "postindustrial" society. Earlier, we outlined some of its essential features. Kerr's forecast of more affluence, leisure, and freedom is typical.

> The industrial society and individual freedom...are not necessarily to be regarded as antagonists. A high degree of discipline in the work place imposed by a web of rules and a large range of governmental activities is fully consistent with a larger freedom for the individual in greater leisure, greater

range of choice in occupations and place of residence, a greater range of alternatives in goods and services on which to use income, and a very wide range of subgroups or associations in which to choose participation.[4]

Kerr's view of the future is consistent with virtually all the major descriptions of the postindustrial society. Material advance and mobility are seen as an expansion of freedom — more choice in goods, occupation, residential location, and affiliation.

The postindustrial society is one presumably to be given over to professional elites who, because of their technical indispensability, are able to demand higher salaries, better working conditions, and more power.

> Eventually not an individual but a complex of scientists, engineers and technicians; of sales, advertising and marketing men; of public relations experts, lobbyists, lawyers and men with specialized knowledge of the Washington bureaucracy and its manipulation; and of coordinators, managers and executives becomes the guiding intelligence of the business firm.[5]

These technical and professional roles have been collectively described by Galbraith as the "technostructure." A full understanding of emerging bureaucratic values and the prospects for personal development requires that the subelements of the technostructure be distinguished. The "coordinators, managers and executives" in organizations are the managerial elites, with direct power and authority over line workers. Their job is to make sure workers are committed and motivated and also to coordinate the efforts of individuals, groups, and organizational subunits. A second major bureaucratic elite, the program staff, plays a different role. They are primarily concerned with providing quality standards for performance of functions and roles in the operating core of the organization as well as for doing the planning necessary to successfully adapt to emerging market, economic, legal, and political conditions. These analysts serve the organization by affecting the work of others.

They are removed from the operating work flow—they may design it, plan it, change it, or train the people who do it, but they do not do it themselves.[6]

Within the program staff are three subgroups having different orientations: work study analysts (such as industrial engineers) who standardize work processes; planning and control analysts (such as long-range planners, budget analysts, and accountants) who standardize outputs; and personnel analysts who standardize skills.[7] The third major element of the technostructure, the support staff, is distinguished from the other groups by the fact that it is not directly supportive of operations. Public and industrial relations, research and development, payroll, food services, legal aid, and so on are examples of units that are not concerned with standardization, as is the program staff. They provide services to the organization that could be purchased externally.

Significantly, it is the support staff and program staff that are the fastest growing components of large organizations since 1950.[8] The growth in these staffs provides the basis for much of the optimism of postindustrial theory. Methods of coordination in the program and support staffs depend less on hierarchical authority than is the case within the operating line. Staff units depend more on horizontal communication and influence among professional peers to achieve coordination and control. In addition, personnel in staff roles are heavily dependent on continuous advanced training, rather than the narrow, low-skill specialization characteristic of older style bureaucratic organizations.

> Much of the program staff work of the organization—for example operations research and industrial engineering—is professional in nature; that is, it involves complex skills and knowledge that can be learned formally. Similarly, many of the jobs in support staff—legal council, researchers, industrial relations specialists, are professional, requiring extensive training.[9]

Managerial elites who control the operating line, on the other hand, need not be highly educated because the required skills are not codified sufficiently for transmission through formal education. Experience and working up the hierarchical ladder are relatively more important where tasks are not well understood. It is not simply the size of the technostructure that has enlarged but also its power.

It is generally conceded that horizontal decentralization is intensifying in modern organizations and that the program staff has been the power beneficiary of this process at the expense of managerial elites, particularly middle managers. The power of staff units has grown with the growth of multidivisional organization. Chandler notes that

> the modern business enterprise is defined by two major characteristics. First it contains many distinct operating units, each with its own administrative offices, its own full time salaried manager and its own set of books and accounts that can be audited separately from those of the larger enterprise. Theoretically, each could operate as an independent business enterprise. The modern multi-unit enterprise has come to operate in different locations, often carrying out a number of economic activities and producing or selling several lines of goods or services.[10]

Under these circumstances, direct hierarchical supervision may be physically impossible or technically impracticable. The consequences of this decentralization for workers in the operating line are significant.

THE WEAKENING OF HIERARCHY AS A CENTRAL BUREAUCRATIC VALUE

The primary vehicle for managerial control of line workers, as noted above, is direct managerial supervision through observation and the monitoring of subordinate activity. Interpersonal relations and skills, the ability to communicate, to get along, to recognize and deal with personality differences are essential elements of skilled management. Earlier we noted Thompson's characterization of this style as "false personalism." The style and vehicle for control over the operating line exercised by the program and support staffs is very different and encourages substantially different values. There may be very little physical interaction between the controlling program staff and the bulk of employees in the operating departments. Control by staff is exercised rather by standardizing skills and program characteristics.

Older forms of enterprise were single-unit operations that undertook a single economic function, producing or selling a single line of products or services. Under the new divisionalized forms of organization, direct supervision (and subordination) is not an effective method of coordination. The operating subunits are simply too diverse in their technologies, planning requirements, and operating styles. As a consequence, the transition to multi-unit organization was accompanied by a movement to the use of subunit output standardization as the major instrument of control and coordination. Rather than attempting to control the operation of subunits on a day-to-day basis through direct supervision, control would be exercised intermittently through the use of performance standards for each subunit. It is reliance on these standards that is shifting power from line managers to those who develop and monitor the standards, the program staff.

> Who surrenders power to the analysts? Obviously, those whose work is standardized, such as the operator who loses the power to choose his work process and the manager who loses the power to decide on his unit's outputs. But so, too, do the managers of these people ... their jobs become institutionalized, technocratic standardization replacing their power of direct supervision."[11]

This shift in power to the staff units serves to further centralize the distribution of top-down control in the operating core of organizations, where most employees work. The power of middle managers is reduced while managers at the very top, utilizing the control systems developed by the staff, direct and coordinate operations in the line. The shift in the method of control from direct supervision to standardization of work process and to subunit output standards greatly weakens the relationship between supervisors and line workers. Supervisors and their middle-level managers have little discretionary authority to make adjustments to meet individualized needs of subordinates. From the perspective of the subordinate, one is subject to plans and standards developed by a staff physically and socially remote, making the relationship with one's superior less significant. Both the supervised and the supervisor may agree that change is difficult because of the remoteness of the staff and the concentration of power at the highest levels of the managerial hierarchy.

Prior to the advent of powerful staffs, subordinates might be uncomfortable in a rigidly hierarchical set of relationships with their superiors. Yet this feeling was mitigated somewhat by the knowledge that superiors could act with authority. The coming of powerful technostructures changed this in a serious way: while hierarchical relationships became less sharp, little satisfaction resulted since impersonality increased in severity.

POSTINDUSTRIAL THEORY AND PRACTICE

The growth of large divisionalized bureaucracies with a dominant staff, allied with a small number of managerial elites, is the reality of emerging bureaucracies. Postindustrial writers have not emphasized these changes, however, but rather have used developments within staff units as models of emerging bureaucratic structures and values. For example, "matrix management" is one of the latest and most widely discussed models of organization.

Matrix management is considered necessary in complex, high technology projects because single, fixed hierarchies are unable to provide the necessary expertise and coordination. The complexity of certain high-technology areas requires diverse forms of expertise, the combination of which may vary radically from one project to another. Owing to the ever shifting combination of technological needs, matrix management requires that subordinates have more than one boss and that they participate in more than one hierarchy.[12]

Davis and Lawrence indicate that a matrix demands new behavior, attitudes, skills, and knowledge.[13] In matrix organizations, conflict is more likely to be on the surface because there is no single boss to resolve conflicting demands. Differences must be resolved between individuals from different functional specialties who hold different attitudes and orientations. A "confrontation/problem-solving" attitude is encouraged, indeed required. Once confrontation has taken place, individuals must be willing to abandon a position that is not supported by the facts. Adaptability, flexibility, and a willingness to confront others become key qualities. Matrix management and organization are not usually found in the operating core of multidivisional organizations. It is much more likely to be found in the program staff and in the supporting staff. It is most likely to be found where there is a need to process complex information and to share specialized expertise. Coordination and control is achieved in the operating core by standardization, but in staff units and support staff, a less hierarchical, more collegial yet competitive atmosphere is necessary.

We have argued that hierarchy and impersonality are potentially destructive of need satisfaction in family, school, and polity. The reduced emphasis on hierarchy and the greater emphasis on willingness to confront others would seem to be positive developments. This optimistic postindustrial image of the future would seem to be in process of confirmation. But is it?

Unfortunately, only a tiny fraction of the work force is in technostructure-type occupations. Hierarchical subordination of a new and more impersonal form is as real today for most workers as it was when organizations had simpler hierarchies. Evidence of this is provided by data on trends in the occupational structure. There has been a steady increase in professional/technical occupations such as accountants, computer specialists, engineers, physicians, and scientists. There has been a parallel decrease in blue-collar occupations such as artisans, machine operators, and laborers. The average annual increase in professional and technical occupations between 1960 and 1977 has been about 3.6 percent, while operatives have declined by 3 percent. These are trends in support of the postindustrial argument emphasizing the growth of technostructure occupations.

The most dramatic shift in the occupational structure, however, is the decline in farming occupations from 17 percent in 1940 to 3 percent in 1979. Also, while the growth in professional/technical occupations has been substantial, an equally large growth has taken place among low-skill, white-collar clerical workers such as bookkeepers, cashiers, secretaries, and office clerks. Indeed, clerical occupations have grown faster than any other, constituting 8 percent more of the work force in 1979 than in 1940.[14] The manual blue-collar occupations have declined 8 percent in the last forty years, but they are still the largest occupational group by far, constituting 32 percent of the workforce in 1979. If one combines manual and clerical occupations, one can easily see that a majority of workers are in relatively low-skill, nontechnostructure occupations.

The postindustrialists have also advanced the argument that sophisticated technologies require a highly educated workforce. In fact, however, the median educational attainment of professional and technical occupations has remained relatively constant since 1948 at 16 years. There have been some gains among managers (from 12.2 to 13.5 years), but the greatest gains have been among relatively low-skill service occupations, from 8.7 years in 1948 to 12.2 in 1977. Educational levels seem to have become somewhat independent of occupation, average levels growing among the low-status occupations but remaining constant among technostructure occupations. Measuring technostructure occupations in terms of rate of growth exaggerates their importance, but there also has been insufficient consideration of the types of industries where technostructure occupations have grown most rapidly.

Manufacturing is becoming a less important source of employment while services are increasing in importance. This shift has important implications for the power environment of work settings and therefore the content of bureaucratic values.

The heaviest concentration (38 percent) of professional/ technical occupations is in the service sector of the economy. This is much more than any other industrial area and much larger than the 11 percent found in manufacturing. In 1970 approximately 7.5 million professional/technical workers were found in service industries, while only 2 million were found in the manufacturing sector. Given the general expansion of service sector employment and contraction in the manufacturing sector, it is reasonable to project a substantial expansion of professional/ technical occupations in the service sector. This growth does not necessarily mean that there has been a concomitant growth in the strategic importance and power of professionals, as the postindustrialists have predicted.

The greatest growth in capital assets has been in the manufacturing sector of the economy, moving from $605 billion in 1940 to $612.9 billion in 1970 or $3.1 million per corporate enterprise in manufacturing. Service corporations have grown more rapidly in terms of total employment, but they are not capital intensive, the average corporate service establishment in 1970 having assets of only $200,000.

The general trend is growth in professional/technicals as predicted, but there are indications that they are working in relatively small settings and not directly in relation to large concentrations of productive assets. In a literal sense, most find themselves in a service relation to industry. This thesis is strengthened by the findings of Eli Ginzberg,[15] who distinguishes those occupations that render services to people from those that render services to business, government, and non-profit organizations. Based on 1970 census data, Ginzberg found that professionals rendering services to organizations are outnumbered approximately two to one by professionals providing services directly to people. Unfortunately, data are not presented indicating the relative patterns of growth of these two groups. Overall, it is probably safe to conclude that the relative growth of professional/technicals in large organizations will not be as great as in smaller organizations.

A third group of professional/technicals are neither in the direct employ of large manufacturing firms nor members of small firms providing services to people. Rather they have relations to large organizations similar in many respects to those of blue-collar workers. Hiring is usually for fixed terms under specified contractual conditions, with their evaluation depending upon specified performance criteria. They are found in relatively small service firms either independent of manufacturing or related to them through contractual agreements. The professional's organizational base is entirely outside the corporate structure of industry, a pattern also applying to large public organizations.

These contractors are of many types, the most important being contractors for military equipment. Also important are the professional consulting firms that provide technical advice on policy matters to government officials. The case of governmental consultants is instructive because they can be properly characterized, in most cases, as "professionals without power." Professional consultants in government do not determine or even substantially influence policy. Rather, their expertise is more often used to justify and elaborate positions held by policy makers in administrative agencies.[16] For most Americans, then, there is little indication that the subordination of earlier periods is likely to end. The adaptability, power, and openness characteristic of the technostructure in large manufacturing establishments is likely to be relevant only to a small occupational elite for the foreseeable future.

Control through the "false personalism" of the line supervisor gives way to the rules, regulations, and operating standards of the technostructure. Remoteness and impersonalism breed a sense of ambiguity and an erosion of legitimacy uncharacteristic of the earlier periods of bureaucratic power. The older forms of hierarchy, false personalism, and specialization provided a relatively concrete set of values and certain institutional paths for their achievement and reinforcement. The emerging era threatens to transform the basis of bureaucratic power from "willing acceptance" to compliance based on extrinsic reward. Some of this can be seen in Michael Maccoby's book "The Gamesman," an attempt to characterize the manager in the modern, large multidivisional organization.[17]

VALUES WITHOUT COMMITMENT — THE MANAGER AS A GAMESMAN

Managerial survival requires that a balance of power be maintained between a shifting set of hierarchies. These areas of competition might be found within major components of the organization (viz., the operating line) but they might also reflect the different interests and orientations between those components — such as the struggle of the technostructure to gain compliance of middle management. Older-style monocratic hierarchies possessed a type of stability in the patterns of organizational control frequently absent in modern organizations. The values that are likely to emerge in these circumstances emphasize "persuasion and seduction rather than heavy and arbitrary commands."[18]

In the uncertain and shifting power environment of emerging organizations, overall organizational goals may be obscure or too complex to be readily understood. As a result, the pursuit of power and of winning political struggles become central preoccupations. Guile and deception, which are a necessary part of the political process, come to be expected, if not positively valued. Somewhat ironically, a sense of equality is expressed in these circumstances. Maccoby has suggested that the gamesman is fair.

> The gamesman has welcomed the era of rights and equal opportunity as both a fair and efficient climate for moving the "best" to the top. In part the sense of fairness comes from the detachment from substantive goals. Final commitments to particular ends or principles are less important than being flexible, adaptive, being able to put together a dominant coalition which can control organizational policy.[19]

It may well be that the prominence of the gamesman is declining as power and influence shift to the technostructure and supporting staff. Indeed, part of the reason for the shift is the adverse consequences of gamesmanlike behavior. Inevitably, the lack of commitment to organizational goals becomes apparent. The shifting posture of the gamesman leads to lack of trust and cooperation in the organization. If it is to maintain internal coordination, a complex organization must be able to generate accurate and reliable information and communicate it quickly and efficiently. The tendency of the gamesman to politicize relations creates a sense of distrust, which in turn blocks and distorts information. The gamesman is a manager, not a planner. Managers deal with the short term, the incremental, not the long range nor even the entire system in the short range.

The meaning of bureaucratic values has been transformed for managers, but what of those whose positions are at the lower levels of the hierarchy? Are the complexity and change that are transforming values at the higher levels of organizational life also transforming them below?

EROSION OF TRUST IN BUREAUCRATIC VALUES
AT THE BOTTOM

Hierarchy in organizations has two faces. The first is the opportunity for occupational mobility with related status and economic rewards, the second is as an instrument of control. Control has been accepted, in part, because of the promise of mobility, or at least the feeling that if one worked hard and had talent, one would be treated fairly—that is, rewarded with mobility in the organization. Yankelovich sums up what he calls the old work values that dominated the workplace roughly up to 1970.

> If women could afford to stay home and not work at a paid job, they did so. As long as a job provided a man with a decent living and some degree of economic security, he would put up with its drawbacks because it meant that he could fulfill his economic obligations to his family and confirm his own self esteem as breadwinner and good provider. The incentive system—mainly money and status rewards—was successful in motivating most people. People were tied to their jobs not only by bonds of commitment to their family, but also loyalty to their organization.[20]

There is some agreement that these values no longer dominate the workplace. Cooper et al.[21] argue that a consensus is emerging that there has been a shift in the attitudes and values of the United States workforce and that this shift has been accompanied by increased dissatisfaction with many aspects of work. To the global question, "How would you rate this company as a place to work compared with what it was when you started here?" there was a 25 percent drop in 1960 to 1977 among clerical workers responding "better now than it was." A similar decline has occurred among all types of employees in regard to rating the fairness of one's company in dealing with employees. While supervisors have improved in their ratings, there has been a very sharp decline in the perception that the company does something in response to employee complaints and problems. The evidence suggests that employee material interests are perceived to be somewhat better fulfilled and that supervisors are more skilled in human relations. But in the end employees are substantially less satisfied and less convinced that their company is fair or responsive to their needs.

These changes may reflect actual changes in work conditions or changes in the expectations of workers about what values work should satisfy. There is no clear answer to which of these factors is most important, but there is evidence that changes at work and in individual workers are important.

We have already noted that workers, at least those in lower-status occupations, are much more educated than their earlier counterparts. Along with greater education is the expectation that work should utilize the skills learned in school. If these opportunities are not provided, the result is likely to be job dissatisfaction, withdrawal from work, and a greater preoccupation with leisure. In a recent survey, Yankelovich found that when work and leisure are compared as sources of satisfaction, only one out of five stated that work means more than leisure. The majority (60 percent) said that while they enjoy their work, it is not their major source of satisfaction. For lower-level workers, bureaucratic hierarchical values are likely to become less salient in comparison to interests outside of work, be they family, sports, or leisure. The primary value of work will be to meet material needs.

The nature of bureaucratic values in large multidivisional organizations cannot be taken as the only or even the most important setting for the transmission of bureaucratic power and values to the larger society. As has been suggested, an increasingly large part of the work force is employed in services and in wholesale and retail trade, where the organizational settings tend to be much smaller and less complex and their environments uncertain.

BUREAUCRATIC VALUES IN NONINDUSTRIAL SECTORS

Galbraith has noted that

> services are rightly assumed to be the domain of the small firm
> and thus of the market system. This in turn has been taken by
> determined defenders of the market to prove that the market-
> controlled economy is not only surviving but resurgent. On ex-
> amination this development turns out to be a good deal more
> complex. Numerous service enterprises are the by-product of
> the rise of the large firm. They are, in effect, a subsidiary and
> supporting the development of the industrial system. This is
> especially the case with that part of the service sector which is
> expanding most rapidly.[22]

The small firm in the service economy certainly cannot be ignored because service occupations are one of the most rapidly
expanding sectors. From the perspective of bureaucratic power,
the issue is to determine whether this sector is subject to bureaucratic value diffusion. If so, are the service sector's structure
and values essentially bureaucratic in traditional ways or does it
represent a wholly new departure?

Some have argued that the expansion of the service sector
represents a diminished role for bureaucratic power and values
in society and a return to the autonomy and independence of
small community-based firms that had little need for hierarchical control mechanisms and that emphasized personal relationships. Services to people cannot be easily standardized, and
therefore they are not effectively and efficiently provided by
large complex organizations. Smaller firms are better able to respond to local community values and local taste. While these
observations have substantial validity, new forms of bureaucratic coordination and control seem to be emerging that allow
the expansion of bureaucratic power into these previously
autonomous spheres. In recent years there has been a rapid expansion of hybrid organizations, the most typical form being
that of the franchise.

Franchises are a product of private small-scale entrepreneurship and corporate planning and control. The entrepreneur provides a substantial measure of capital as well as energy and intelligence, while the corporation provides advertising and some capital and technical assistance. In effect, the operating core in franchise operations is severed from the corporation, thereby eliminating the organizational hierarchy as the primary mechanism of control. Control and coordination are assured through the operating standards and technical assistance provided by the corporation and embodied in contractual agreements.

As in the case of large complex organizations, control is achieved less by day-to-day hierarchical commands than by periodic monitoring by corporate representatives of contract compliance. There is a degree of increased autonomy in these arrangements that does not exist in hierarchical control systems. In principle, there is greater room for day-to-day flexibility in the details of task execution because of the nature of the contractual relationship and also because of the physical absence of an overhead hierarchy. Communications and feedback are relatively rapid, again because of the small scale of operations at decentralized locations. However, these elements of flexibility and autonomy are constrained by rigid performance and quality standards within narrowly specified product or service lines. It is only by narrowing the scope of organizational products and services that it is possible to effectively control operations from remote locations.

For the industrial worker, problems of control and personal fulfillment could be attached to a clearly visible hierarchy of organizational authority. For those in the service sector and in retail trade, the supervisory hierarchy may end with the local franchise owner. As the worker looks upward, he or she sees a very flat hierarchy, with perhaps only a manager and owner above; the worker's major interactions are with coworkers and customers. In some regards, then, workers in service industries are in a different position than those in manufacturing. Supervisory relations are less complex and perhaps more personal. But workers in these areas share with their manufacturing counterparts the fundamental problems of little control over the content of their job tasks and even less opportunity for mobility or managerial responsiveness. Under these circumstances, one finds very low levels of work commitment and trust in the organization.

Since at least the 1930s, corporate management has believed that it is essential for workers to accept the organization's premises about the prerogatives of the hierarchy, the advantages of specialization, and the centrality of work. Given the lack of trust in the organization by workers, how bureaucratic values will be diffused has become increasingly problematic. The management issue is how to successfully diffuse bureaucratic values and how to reestablish trust and thereby reestablish the legitimacy of bureaucratic power.

CHANGES IN PRIMARY INSTITUTIONS AND NEW PROBLEMS OF BUREAUCRATIC LEGITIMATION

The efforts and methods to reestablish trust and legitimacy are just now emerging. Diffusion in the past has relied on shaping the character of the family, school, and polity. These in turn have reinforced the values of hierarchy, specialization, and impersonality. When the idea of hierarchy was still regarded as central to bureaucratic functioning, interpersonal skill or "false personalism" emerged as an attribute to be nurtured in the school and family.

Technical reports and accounting procedures are important in multidivisional and service industries. In principle, this would imply a shift away from building interpersonal skills and a renewed emphasis on basic mathematical and language skills in schools. The impersonal character of communications requires greater technical precision in both quantitative and nonquantitative communication.

It is unlikely that old-fashioned hierarchies in schools will reassert themselves because they do not model workplaces. Rather, there is likely to be a growing emphasis on student performance standards that might be raised using a variety of teaching formats and methods. Indeed, in some states this approach is now required of local schools by the state. Students failing to achieve mandated performance standards are not passed to the next grade. These standards are established by state education departments and enforced through uniform testing and statewide monitoring of the results.

The use of performance standards and monitoring in schools is strikingly similar to patterns in the industrial sector. Significantly, performance standards are used not only to evaluate individual students but also to evaluate the performance of individual schools and school districts in a manner much like the evaluation of subunits in multidivisional corporations. Unlike earlier attempts to reform schools, there is less concern to prescribe the specifics of school organizational structure; performance and monitoring are central.

These developments could have a positive impact on the quality of schools insofar as routines and control receive less emphasis and basic skills—reading, mathematics, and writing—receive more emphasis. How in fact these new systems are to be judged depends on the substantive content of the performance criteria. There is some evidence that there will be pressures to establish very narrow and specialized basic skills. This is illustrated in those states where basic skills are defined in terms of the ability to balance a checkbook, read a clock or bus schedule, and do comparison shopping at the local supermarket. How skills will be defined will probably depend on the class position of the school population. Schools in middle- and upper-class areas will emphasize fundamental mathematical and language skills, while those in lower-class areas will emphasize narrow technical skills and performance standards.

The implications of the emerging bureaucratic forms for the family are somewhat more dramatic than for schools. There are no signs that the tendency for households to decrease in size and parental authority will change. (For example, in 1978 single-parent households constituted 17 percent of all households.) These trends have intensified so much that many authorities are questioning the capacity of the family to play an effective socialization role.

The weakness of the family in performing its socialization functions is even recognized by industry, whose response has been to add "family-like" structures to organizations. The clearest examples are the provision of child care, help in relocation, and job and career counseling. These supports are thought to reduce employee stress and to improve morale and productivity.

At best, these accommodations by industry are helpful in meeting the basic care needs of families. However, they are not likely to reach the essential problem of providing emotional support to children. Perhaps a humanistic atmosphere at work can be a partial substitute for the warmth of a nuclear or extended family, but absent parents cannot provide it. Increasingly, children seek the warmth and support of other children because of the physical and psychological absence of their parents. This obviously presents a major threat to their own well-being but also ironically to industry, which traditionally has depended on the family to socialize children to bureaucratic values. The growth in distrust of work institutions and the lack of commitment of workers to their jobs might be seen as a failure of socialization.

Our model of the political system assumes that it should provide opportunities to set goals for the society. It assumes citizens who are socialized in the family and school to recognize the importance of these public roles and to provide the basic knowledge and values required for the intelligent and compassionate exercise of the rights of citizenship. Elitist rule is hardly consistent with this process. Popular political discussion of control and participation in the political system is shifting from the issue of whether the polity is more or less participatory to the question of bringing adequate resources to bear on mounting social and economic problems, be that system participatory or nonparticipatory. Welfare rolls have expanded in proportion to the deterioration in families, while the increase in the costs of law enforcement parallels the increase in crime rates. Indeed, a consensus seems to be emerging that even the dependency of the aged can no longer be averted by governmental programs and income support. Without doubt governmental structures have become less participatory, but this is less important than the fact that government is unable to deal with basic material needs. Again, there is some irony in these developments, because industry has traditionally depended on government to assist in the diffusion of bureaucratic values and relatedly to assure the legitimacy of institutional arrangements for business enterprise. It is not that government is a less willing servant as that it is perhaps a less capable servant. The inescapable conclusion is that government and family are both less effective aids to the legitimation of bureaucratic power, with consequent crises of trust and legitimacy.

The future of bureaucratic power and personal need satisfaction is clouded by complex cross-currents. The declining legitimacy of bureaucratic power could be regarded as a liberating development because it frees individuals to consciously consider the balance of incentives and contributions associated with bureaucratic power rather than to simply accept hierarchical structures without question.

Unfortunately, the decline in the legitimacy of bureaucratic power has been associated with a weakening ability of industrial bureaucracies to meet material needs, with family arrangements that are increasingly unable to provide adequate emotional support to children, and with a political system that is less controllable by its citizens and even less capable of supporting material needs.

Notes

1. Bureaucratic Power and Personal Development

1. Harvey Wheeler, *Democracy in a Revolutionary Era* (Santa Barbara: Center for the Study of Democratic Institutions, 1970), pp. 99-100.
2. Charles Reich, *The Greening of America* (New York: Bantam Books, 1971), pp. 7-8.
3. Michael Crozier, *The World of the Office Worker* (New York: Schocken Books, 1973), pp. ix-x.
4. Abraham H. Maslow, *Toward a Psychology of Being* (New York: Van Nostrand, 1962), p. 97.
5. Peter Blau, *Exchange and Power in Social Life* (New York: Oxford, 1973), pp. 150-51.
6. Ibid., pp. 21-22.
7. Ibid., p. 22.

2. Bureaucratic Values and Personal Needs

1. See *From Max Weber: Essays in Sociology*, edited and translated by H.H. Gerth and C. Wright Mills (Oxford: Oxford Univ. Press, 1946).

2. Szymon Chodak, *Societal Development* (New York: Oxford, 1973), pp. 150-51.
3. Kenneth McNeil, "Understanding Organizational Power: Building on the Weberian Legacy," *Administrative Science Quarterly,* 23 (Mar. 1978), pp. 69-75.
4. A general discussion of Maslow in the larger context of personal development can be found in Jeanne N. Knutson, *The Human Basis of the Polity* (Chicago: Aldine, 1972), pp. 23-106.
5. Ibid., p. 26.
6. Ibid., p. 30.
7. Ibid., p. 48.
8. Ibid., p. 51.
9. Ibid., p. 92.
10. *Work in America,* Report of a Special Task Force to the Secretary of Health, Education and Welfare (Cambridge: MIT Press, 1973), p. 21.
11. Victor A. Thompson, *Modern Organizations* (New York: Knopf, 1969), chs. 2-4.
12. Peter Blau, *Exchange and Power in Social Life* (New York: Oxford, 1973), p. 146.
13. Robert Presthus, *The Organizational Society* (New York: St. Martin's Press, 1978), pp. 184-88.
14. Ibid., pp. 143-83.
15. Thompson, *Modern Organizations,* p. 93.
16. Ibid., p. 94.

3. THE DIFFUSION OF BUREAUCRATIC VALUES

1. Jacob L. Gewirtz, "Mechanisms of Social Learning: Some Roles of Stimulation and Behavior in Early Human Development," in *Handbook of Socialization Theory and Research,* edited by David A. Goslin (Chicago: Rand McNally, 1971).
2. Ibid., p. 140.
3. Ibid., p. 152.
4. United States Bureau of the Census, *Statistical Abstract of the United States: 1971,* p. 108.
5. Michael B. Katz, *Class, Bureaucracy, and Schools* (New York: Praeger, 1971), pp. 1-5.

6. Ibid., p. xxiii.
7. Joseph C. Grannis, "The School as a Model of Society," in *The Learning of Political Behavior,* edited by Norman Adler and Charles Harrington (Glenview, Ill.: Scott, Foresman, 1970), pp. 137-48.
8. Ibid., p. 141.
9. Ibid., p. 142.
10. Donald Gilbert McKinley, *Social Class and Family Life* (New York: Free Press, 1964), p. 129.
11. Daniel R. Miller and Guy E. Swanson, *The Changing American Parent* (New York: Wiley, 1958).
12. Ibid., p. 39.
13. Ibid., p. 35.
14. Melvin L. Kohn, *Class and Conformity* (Homewood, Ill.: Dorsey Press, 1969).
15. Frances Fox Piven and Richard A. Cloward, *Regulating the Poor* (New York: Vintage Books, 1971).
16. Ibid., p. 166.
17. Ibid., pp. 171-72.
18. Anthony Downs, *Inside Bureaucracy* (Boston: Little, Brown, 1967), ch. 19.
19. Ibid., p. 237.
20. Philip Selznick, *TVA and the Grass Roots* (New York: Harper and Row, 1966), p. 29.
21. Ibid., p. 220.

4. DIFFUSION IN INDUSTRIAL AND POSTINDUSTRIAL SOCIETIES

1. Reinhard Bendix, *Work and Authority in Industry: Ideologies of Management in the Course of Industrialization* (New York: Harper Torch Books, 1963), ch. 2.
2. Ibid., p. 24, citing Paul Mantoux, *The Industrial Revolution in the Eighteenth Century* (New York: Harcourt, Brace, 1927), pp. 86-87.
3. Ibid., p. 25, citing P. Gaskell, *The Manufacturing Population of England* (London: Baldwin and Cradock, 1833), p. 45.
4. Ibid., p. 26, citing M. Beer, ed., *Life of Robert Owen* (New York: Knopf, 1920), p. 150.

5. Ibid., p. 38.
6. Ibid., p. 99.
7. Ibid., p. 53.
8. Ibid., p. 105.
9. U.S. Bureau of the Census, *Historical Statistics of the United States: Colonial Times to 1957* (Washington, D.C.: U.S. Government Printing Office, 1956), p. 573.
10. Ibid., p. 413.
11. Peter Blau, "A Formal Theory of Differentiation in Organizations," *American Sociological Review*, 35 (Apr. 1970), pp. 201-18.
12. Ibid., pp. 204-5.
13. Ibid., p. 213.
14. Melvin Kohn, "Bureaucratic Man: A Portrait and an Interpretation," *American Sociological Review,* 36 (June 1971), pp. 461-74.
15. Robert Lerner, *Management Control and the Large Corporation* (New York: Dunellon, 1970), p. 27.
16. J.M. Pahl and R.E. Pahl, *Managers and Their Wives* (London: Allen Lane, Penguin, 1971), pp. 50-51.
17. Ibid., p. 64.
18. Franklin P. Kilpatrick, Milton C. Cummings, Jr., and M. Kent Jennings, *Source Book of a Study of Occupational Values and the Image of the Federal Service* (Washington, D.C.: Brookings Institution, 1964), p. 91.
19. Eric Trist, "Urban North America: The Challenge of the Next Thirty Years," in *Organizational Frontiers and Human Values,* edited by Warren Schmidt (Belmont, Calif.: Wadsworth, 1970), p. 77.
20. Warren G. Bennis, *American Bureaucracy* (San Francisco: Aldine, 1970), p. 166.
21. Ibid.
22. Ibid., p. 170.
23. Arnold S. Tannenbaum et al., *Hierarchy in Organizations* (San Francisco: Jossey-Bass, 1974).
24. Ibid., p. 84.
25. Ibid.

26. Ibid.
27. Ibid., p. 91.

5. MODELS OF PRIMARY INSTITUTIONS

1. Gaetano Mosca, *The Ruling Class* (New York: McGraw-Hill, 1939), p. 50.
2. Stanley Allen Renshon, *Psychological Needs and Political Behavior* (London: Free Press, 1974), pp. 124-25.
3. Robert Dreeban, *On What Is Learned in School* (Reading, Mass.: Addison-Wesley, 1968), p. 105.
4. Thomas R. Dye and H. Zeigler, *The Irony of Democracy,* 2d ed. (Belmont, Calif.: Duxbury Press, 1972), p. 363.
5. Ibid., p. 366.
6. Ibid., p. 368.
7. W. Kornhauser, *The Politics of Mass Society* (Glencoe, Ill.: Free Press, 1959), p. 33.
8. Seymour Lipset, *Political Man* (Garden City, N.Y.: Doubleday, 1960), pp. 101-2.
9. Urie Bronfenbrenner, "Socialization and Social Class Through Time and Space," in *Readings in Social Psychology*, 3d ed., edited by E.C. Maccoby, T.M. Newcomb, and E.L. Hartley (New York: Holt, Rinehart, and Winston, 1958), p. 419.
10. Melvin Kohn, "Social Class and Parent Child Relationships," *American Journal of Sociology*, 68 (Jan. 1963), pp. 471-80.
11. Edward Z. Dager, "Socialization and Personality Development in the Child," in *Handbook of Marriage and the Family*, edited by Harold T. Christensen (Chicago: Rand McNally, 1964), p. 773.
12. R.P. Stukert, "Occupational Mobility and Family Relationships," *Social Forces,* 41 (Mar. 1963), pp. 301-7.
13. Peter Rossi, *Why Families Move: A Study in the Social Psychology of Urban Residential Mobility* (Glencoe, Ill.: Free Press, 1955).
14. Dager, "Socialization," p. 775.
15. Grannis, "School as a Model," in Christiansen, p. 138.
16. John Dewey, as cited in Grannis, "School as a Model," pp. 34-36.
17. Grannis, "School as a Model," p. 139.

6. The Bureaucratization of the Family

1. U.S. Bureau of the Census, *Historical Statistics of the United States, Colonial Times to 1970,* Series A288-319, A320-344, and A345-349.
2. Michael Anderson, "Mean Household Size in England Since the Sixteenth Century," in *Household and Family in Past Time,* edited by Peter Laslett and Richard Wall (Cambridge: Cambridge Univ. Press, 1972), pp. 125-57.
3. Ibid., p. 139.
4. Michael Anderson, "Household Structure and the Industrial Revolution: Mid-nineteenth-century Preston in Comparative Perspective," in Laslett and Wall, *Household and Family,* p. 221.
5. Ibid., p. 222.
6. Daniel Nelson, *Managers and Workers* (Madison: Univ. of Wisconsin Press, 1975), p. 80.
7. Ibid., pp. 83-84.
8. Ibid., p. 86.
9. Ibid., pp. 149-50.
10. Ibid., p. 12.
11. Bert Adams, *The American Family* (Chicago: Markham, 1971), pp. 62, 64.
12. Herman Lantz, Martin Schultz, and Mary O'Hara, "The Changing American Family from the Preindustrial to the Industrial Period: A Final Report," *American Sociological Review,* 42 (June 1977), p. 407.
13. Ibid.
14. Ibid.
15. Ibid.
16. Lois Hoffman and F. Ivan Nye, *Working Mothers* (San Francisco: Jossey-Bass, 1974), p. 11.
17. Ibid., p. 12.
18. Ibid., p. 46.
19. Ibid., p. 173.
20. Ibid., p. 197.
21. Daniel R. Miller and Guy E. Swanson, *The Changing American Parent* (New York: Wiley, 1958), p. 27.

22. Ibid., pp. 27-28.
23. Paul Lawrence and Jay Lorsch, *Developing Organizations* (Reading, Mass.: Addison-Wesley, 1969), p. 26.

7. BUREAUCRACY AND THE EDUCATIONAL CRISIS

1. D.H. Heath, *Humanizing Schools* (New York: Hayden, 1971), p. 44.
2. Ibid., p. 62.
3. Michael B. Katz, *Class, Bureaucracy, and Schools* (New York: Praeger, 1971), p. xviii.
4. Ibid., p. xx.
5. Ibid., p. xxiii.
6. Michael B. Katz, "From Voluntarism to Bureaucracy in American Education," *Sociology of Education,* 44 (Summer 1971), p. 328.
7. Katz, *Class, Bureaucracy, and Schools,* p. 68.
8. Arthur Stinchcombe, "Social Structure and Organizations," in *Handbook of Organizations,* edited by J. March (Chicago: Rand McNally, p. 162.
9. Katz, *Class, Bureaucracy, and Schools,* p. 104.
10. Ivan Illich, "The Breakdown of Schools: A Problem or a Symptom?" in *Childhood and Socialization,* edited by H.P. Dreitzel (New York: Macmillan, 1973), p. 14.
11. Ibid., pp. 314-15.
12. Ibid., p. 323.
13. Ronald G. Corwin, *Sociology of Education* (New York: Appleton-Century-Crofts, 1965), p. 189.
14. Samuel Bowles and Herbert Gintis, *Schooling in Capitalist America* (New York: Basic Books, 1976).
15. Ibid., pp. 130-31.
16. Ibid., p. 148.
17. Ibid., p. 56.
18. Ibid., p. 69.
19. Martin Carnoy, *Education as Cultural Imperialism* (New York: David McKay, 1973), p. 344.
20. Martin Carnoy, *School in a Corporate Society* (New York: David McKay, 1975), pp. 370-71.

21. Carnoy, *Education as Cultural Imperialism,* p. 346.
22. Thorstein Veblen, *The Higher Learning in America* (New York: Huebsch, 1918).
23. Peter M. Blau, *The Organization of Academic Work* (New York: Wiley-Interscience, 1973).
24. Barry D. Anderson, "School Bureaucratization and Alienation from High School," *Sociology of Education,* 46 (Summer 1973), p. 331.
25. Ibid.
26. Ibid., p. 328.
27. Joel H. Spring, *Education and the Rise of the Corporate State* (Boston: Beacon Press, 1972), pp. 164-65.

8. POLITICAL POWER, CULTURE, AND PARTICIPATION

1. C. Wright Mills, *The Power Elite* (New York: Oxford, 1956).
2. Ibid., pp. 8-9.
3. Ibid., p. 289.
4. Ibid., p. 11.
5. Ibid., p. 324.
6. Robert A. Dahl, "A Critique of the Ruling Elite Model," *American Political Science Review,* 52 (June 1958), passim.
7. For an assessment of these and other criticisms of Mills's thesis, see Kenneth Prewitt and Alan Stone, *The Ruling Elites* (New York: Harper and Row, 1973), ch. 4, "The Power Elite Thesis."
8. Quoted in S. Landau, "C. Wright Mills: The Last Six Months," *Ramparts* (Aug. 1965), p. 48.
9. Robert A. Dahl, *Who Governs?* (New Haven: Yale University Press, 1961).
10. An excellent sketch of Dahl's pluralism, together with a summary of the critique of pluralism, is found in David Ricci's *Community Power and Democratic Theory* (New York: Random House, 1971), chs. 7 and 8.
11. Nelson Polsby, "How to Study Community Power," *Journal of Politics* (Aug. 1960), p. 476.
12. Dahl, *Who Governs?,* p. 93.
13. For a full discussion of this important point, see Peter Bachrach and Morton S. Baratz, "Decisions and Non-decisions: An

Analytical Framework," *American Political Science Review*, 57 (Sept. 1963), pp. 641-42.

14. Robert O. Schulze, "The Role of Economic Dominants in Community Power Structure," in *The Structure of Community Power*, edited by Michael Aiken and Paul E. Mott (New York: Random House, 1970), p. 60.

15. Ibid., p. 61.

16. Ibid., p. 63.

17. Ibid., p. 64.

18. Robert A. Dahl, "From Oligarchy to Pluralism: The Patricians and the Entrepreneurs," in Aiken and Mott, *Structure of Community Power,* p. 32.

19. Thomas R. Dye, *Who's Running America? Institutional Leadership in the United States* (Englewood Cliffs, N.J.: Prentice-Hall, 1976), p. 222.

20. Ibid., p. 210.

21. Ibid., p. 211.

22. Ibid., p. 212.

23. G. William Domhoff, *The Higher Circles* (New York: Random House, 1970).

24. Arnold Tannenbaum, *Hierarchy in Organizations* (San Francisco: Josey-Bass, 1974).

25. Gabriel A. Almond, "Comparative Political Systems," *Journal of Politics,* 18 (Aug. 1956), p. 396.

26. Sidney Verba, in *Political Culture and Political Development,* edited by L.W. Pye and S. Verba (Princeton: Princeton University Press, 1965), p. 513.

27. Ibid., p. 516.

28. Gabriel A. Almond and G. Bingham Powell, Jr., *Comparative Politics: A Developmental Approach* (Boston: Little, Brown, 1966), p. 53.

29. Gabriel A. Almond and Sidney Verba, *The Civic Culture* (Boston: Little, Brown, 1965), p. 22.

30. Ibid., p. 30.

31. Ibid.

32. Almond and Powell, *Comparative Politics,* p. 96.

33. U.S. Senate, Committee on Government Operations, *Confidence and Concern: Citizens View American Government, Part*

I (Washington, D.C.: U.S. Government Printing Office, 1973). Tables 8.2 and 8.3 are taken from this report.

34. Norman H. Nie, Sidney Verba, and John R. Petrocik, *The Changing American Voter* (Cambridge: Harvard Univ. Press, 1976), p. 284.

35. Joyce Gelb and Lief Palley, *Tradition and Change in American Party Politics* (New York: Thomas Y. Crowell, 1975), p. 45.

36. U.S. Senate, *Confidence and Concern,* pp. 153-54.

9.   THE EMERGING LOSS OF TRUST AND
LEGITIMACY IN SOCIETY

1. Clark Kerr, John Dunlop, Frederick Harbison, and Charles Myers, *Industrialism and Industrial Man* (Cambridge: Harvard Univ. Press, 1960), pp. 266-67.

2. Ibid., p. 47.

3. Ibid., pp. 18-19.

4. Ibid., p. 267.

5. John Kenneth Galbraith, *Economics and the Public Purpose* (New York: Signet, 1973), p. 78.

6. Henry Mintzberg, *The Structuring of Organizations* (Englewood Cliffs, N.J.: Prentice-Hall, 1979), pp. 29-30.

7. Ibid., pp. 30-31.

8. J.A. Litterer, *The Analysis of Organizations,* 2d ed. (New York: Wiley, 1973), pp. 584-85.

9. Mintzberg, *Structuring of Organizations,* p. 99.

10. Alfred Chandler and Herman Daems, eds., *Managerial Hierarchies* (Cambridge: Harvard Univ. Press, 1980), pp. 9-11.

11. Mintzberg, *Structuring of Organizations,* p. 94.

12. Stanley M. Davis and Paul R. Lawrence, *Matrix* (Reading, Mass.: Addison-Wesley, 1977), p. 107.

13. Ibid., p. 103.

14. U.S. Department of Labor, *1978 Employment and Training Report of the President,* Tables A-16 and A-17.

15. Eli Ginzberg, "The Professionalization of the Workforce," *Scientific American,* 240, 3 (Mar. 1979), pp. 48-53.

16. Marvin C. Alkin, Richard Daillak, and Peter White, *Using Evaluations* (Beverly Hills, Calif.: Sage Pubns., 1979), pp. 235-59.

17. Michael Maccoby, *The Gamesman* (New York: Simon and Schuster, 1976), p. 17.
18. "Leadership Needs of the 1980s," *Current Issues in Higher Education,* 1, 1 (1979), p. 22.
19. Maccoby, *Gamesman,* p. 18.
20. Yankelovich, Daniel, "The New Psychological Contracts at Work," *Psychology Today,* May 1978, p. 47.
21. "Changing Employee Values: Deepening Discontent?" *Harvard Business Review,* Jan./Feb. 1979, p. 119.
22. Galbraith, *Economics and the Public Purpose,* p. 53.

Bibliography

Adams, Bert N. "Isolation, Function, and Beyond: American Kinship in the 1970's." *Journal of Marriage and the Family,* 32 (Nov. 1970): 575-97.

_____. *The American Family.* Chicago: Markham, 1971.

Adizes, Ichak. *Industrial Democracy: Yugoslav Style.* New York: Free Press, 1971.

Adler, Norman, and Charles Harrington, eds. *The Learning of Political Behavior.* Glenview, Ill.: Scott, Foresman, 1970.

Agger, Robert E.; Daniel Goldrich; and Bert E. Swanson. *The Rulers and the Ruled: Political Power and Impotence in American Communities.* New York: Wiley, 1964.

Agger, Robert E., and Marshall N. Goldstein. *Who Will Rule the Schools: A Cultural Class Crisis.* Belmont, Calif.: Wadsworth, 1971.

Agger, Robert E., and Vincent Ostrom. "Political Participation in a Small Community." In *Political Behavior,* edited by H. Eulau, S.J. Eldersveld, and M. Janowitz. Glencoe, Ill.: Free Press, 1956.

Alford, Robert. *Bureaucracy and Participation.* Chicago: Rand McNally, 1969.

Almond, Gabriel A., and G. Bingham Powell, Jr. *Comparative Politics: A Developmental Approach.* Boston: Little, Brown, 1966.

Almond, Gabriel A., and Sidney Verba. *The Civic Culture.* Boston: Little, Brown, 1966.

Altschuler, Alan. *Community Control.* New York: Pegasus, 1970.

Anderson, Chas. W. "Public Policy, Pluralism, and the Further Evolution of Advanced Industrial Society." Paper delivered to the Annual Meeting of the American Political Science Assn., 1973.

Anderson, Michael. *Family Structure in 19th Century Landcashire.* Cambridge, England: University Press, 1971.

Argyris, Chris. *Organization and Innovation.* Homewood, Ill.: Irwin, 1965.

Argyris, Chris. "Some Limits of Rational Man Organizational Theory." *Public Administration Review,* 33 (May/June 1973): 253-67.

Bachrach, Peter. *The Theory of Democratic Elitism: A Critique.* Boston: Little, Brown, 1967.

Bachrach, Peter, and Morton S. Baratz. "Decisions and Non-Decisions: An Analytical Framework." *American Political Science Review,* 57 (Sept. 1963): 632-42.

Bandura, Albert. "Social Learning Theory and Identificatory Processes." In *Handbook of Socialization Theory and Research,* edited by D.A. Goslin. Chicago: Rand McNally, 1971.

Bardis, Panos D. "Family Forms and Variations Historically Considered." In *Handbook of Marriage and the Family,* edited by H.T. Christensen. Chicago: Rand McNally, 1964.

Bay, Christian. " 'Freedom' as a Tool of Oppression." In *The Case for Participatory Democracy,* edited by C.G. Benello and D. Roussopoulos. New York: Viking Press, 1971.

————. *The Structure of Freedom.* Stanford, Calif.: Stanford Univ. Press, 1950.

Becker, Howard S., ed. *Social Problems: A Modern Approach.* New York: Wiley, 1966.

Beldoch, Michael. "The False Psychology of Encounter Groups." *Intellectual Digest,* (Oct. 1971): 85-88.

Bendix, Reinhard. "Bureaucracy and the Problem of Power." Bobbs-Merrill reprint from *Public Administration Review,* 5 (Summer 1945).

_____. *Nation-Building and Citizenship.* New York: Wiley, 1964.

_____. *Work and Authority in Industry.* New York: Harper and Row, 1963.

Benello, C. George, and Dimitros Roussopoulos, eds. *The Case for Participatory Democracy.* New York: Viking Press, 1971.

Bennis, Warren. "The Decline of Bureaucracy and Organizations of the Future." In *Organizational Issues in Industrial Society,* edited by J.M. Shepard. Englewood Cliffs, N.J.: Prentice-Hall, 1972.

Berger, Peter; Briggitte Berger; and Hansfield Kellner. *The Homeless Mind.* New York: Random House, 1973.

Berube, Maurice R., and Marilyn Gittell, eds. *Confrontation at Cogan Hill-Brownsville.* New York: Praeger, 1969.

Birch, A.H. "England and Wales." In *Citizen Participation in Political Life* issue of *International Social Science Journal,* 12, 1 (1960): 15-26.

Blau, Peter M. *Bureaucracy in Modern Society.* New York: Random House, 1956.

_____. *The Organization of Academic Work.* New York: Wiley, 1973.

Blau, Peter M., and W. Richard Scott. *Formal Organizations.* San Francisco: Chandler, 1962.

Blauner, Robert. *Alienation and Freedom.* Chicago: Univ. of Chicago Press, 1964.

Bloom, Samuel W. "The Sociology of Medical Education." *Milbank Memorial Foundation Quarterly,* 43 (Apr. 1965): 143-84.

_____. *The Organizational Revolution.* New York: Harper, 1953.

Bookchin, Murray. "Toward a Liberatory Technology." In *The Case for Participatory Democracy,* edited by C.G. Benello and D. Roussopoulos. New York: Viking Press, 1971.

Boulding, Kenneth. *The Organizational Revolution.* New York: Harper, 1953.

Bowles, Samuel, and Herbert Gintis. *Schooling in Capitalist America.* New York: Basic Books, 1976.

Brody, Grace. "Socioeconomic Differences in Stated Maternal Child-Rearing Practices and in Observed Maternal Behavior." *Journal of Marriage and the Family* (Nov. 1963): 656-60.

Bronfenbrenner, Urie. *Two Worlds of Childhood.* New York: Russell Sage Foundation, 1970.

Burr, Wesley R. *Theory Construction and the Sociology of the Family.* New York: Wiley, 1973.

Campbell, Angus, et al. *The American Voter.* New York: Wiley, 1960.

Campbell, Ernest Q. "Adolescent Socialization." In *Handbook of Socialization Theory and Research,* edited by D.A. Goslin. Chicago: Rand McNally, 1971.

Chandler, Alfred D. *Strategy and Structure.* Cambridge: M.I.T. Press, 1962.

Cherns, A.B. "Work or Life." Section N Presidential Address, The British Association for the Advancement of Science (n.d.).

Cherns, A.B., and L.E. Davis, eds. *The Quality of Working Life.* (San Francisco: Jossey-Bass, 1974.

Christensen, Harold T., ed. *Handbook of Marriage and the Family.* Chicago: Rand McNally, 1964.

Clausen, John A., ed. *Socialization and Society.* Boston: Little, Brown, 1968.

Cohen, David K., and Marvin Lazerson. *Education and the Corporate Order.* Reprint No. 335. Andover, Mass.: Warner Modular Pubns., 1972.

Cole, Robert E. *Japanese Blue Collar.* Berkeley: Univ. of California Press, 1971.

Converse, Philip E. "Change in the American Electorate." In *The Human Meaning of Social Change,* edited by A. Campbell and P.E. Converse. New York: Russell Sage Foundation, 1972.

Converse, Philip E., and Angus Campbell, eds. *The Human Meaning of Social Change.* New York: Russell Sage Foundation, 1972.

Cottrell, Leonard S., Jr. "Interpersonal Interaction and the Development of the Self." In *Handbook of Socialization Theory and Research,* edited by D.A. Goslin. Chicago: Rand McNally, 1971.

Crozier, Michael. "Bureaucratic Organizations and the Evolution of Industrial Society." In *A Sociological Reader on Complex Organizations,* edited by Amitai Etzioni. New York: Holt, Rinehart and Winston, 1969.

_____. *The World of the Office Worker.* Chicago: Univ. of Chicago Press, 1971. (Translated.)

Crozier, Michael, et al. *The Crisis of Democracy.* New York: New York Univ. Press, 1975.

Cuber, John F., with Peggy B. Harroff. *The Significant Americans: A Study of Sexual Behavior among the Affluent.* New York: Appleton-Century-Crofts, 1965.

Cummings, L.L., and W.E. Scott, eds. *Readings in Organizational Behavior and Human Performance.* Homewood, Ill.: Irwin, Dorsey, 1969.

Dager, Edward Z. "Socialization and Personality Development in the Child." In *Handbook of Marriage and the Family,* edited by H.T. Christensen. Chicago: Rand McNally, 1964.

Dahl, Robert A. *After the Revolution.* New Haven: Yale Univ. Press, 1970.

_____. "Further Reflections on 'The Elitist Theory of Democracy.'" *American Political Science Review,* 60 (June 1966): 285.

_____. *Polyarchy.* New Haven: Yale Univ. Press, 1971.

_____. *Who Governs? Democracy and Power in an American City.* New Haven: Yale Univ. Press, 1961.

Dean, Dwight G. "Alienation and Political Apathy." *Social Forces,* 38 (Mar. 1960): 185-89.

Deteriorating Trust in Government — What Was the Impact of Watergate? Ann Arbor, Mich., *Institute for Social Research Newsletter,* 3, 3 (Summer 1975).

de Tocqueville, Alexis. *Democracy in America.* New York: Knopf, 1945.

Deutsch, Steven E., and John Howard, eds. *Where It's At: Radical Perspectives in Sociology.* New York: Harper and Row, 1970.

Devine, Donald J. *The Political Culture of the United States.* Boston: Little, Brown, 1972.

Di Palma, G. *Apathy and Participation.* Glencoe, Ill.: Free Press, 1970.

Dore, Ronald. *British Factory-Japanese Factory.* London: Allen and Unwin, 1973.

Dubin, Robert. "Industrial Worker's Worlds: A Study of the Central Life Interests of Industrial Workers." *Social Problems,* 3 (1956): 131-42.

_____. "Work Attachments, Central Life Interests and the Alienation Myth." Unpublished paper presented at the 70th Annual Meeting, American Sociological Assn., San Francisco, 1975.

Dykes, Archie. *Faculty Participation in Academic Decision Making.* Washington: American Council on Education, 1968.

Eckstein, Harry. *A Theory of Stable Democracy.* Princeton, N.J.: Center for International Studies, 1961.

Edwards, John N. "The Future of the Family Revisited." *Journal of Marriage and the Family* (Aug. 1967): 505-11.

Erlanger, Howard S. "Social Class and Corporal Punishment in Childrearing: A Reassessment." *American Sociological Review,* 39 (Feb. 1974): 68-85.

Ferkiss, Victor. *Technological Man.* New York: George Braziller, 1969.

Finifter, Ada W. "The Friendship Group as a Protective Environment for Political Deviants." *American Political Science Review* (June 1974): 607-25.

Flacks, Richard. "On Participatory Democracy." In *Where It's At: Radical Perspectives in Sociology,* edited by S.E. Deutsch and J. Howard. New York: Harper and Row, 1970.

_____. "On the Uses of Participatory Democracy." *Dissent,* 13 (Nov.-Dec. 1966): 701-8.

Form, William H. "The Internal Stratification of the Working Class: Systems of Involvement of Auto Workers in Four Countries." *American Sociological Review,* 38 (Dec. 1973): 697-711.

_____. "Job Unionism vs. Political Unionism in Four Countries: The Relevance of Industrial Development, Type of Union and Skill Level." *Industrial Relations,* 12 (May 1973): 224-38.

_____. "Occupational and Social Integration of Auto Workers in Four Countries." *International Journal of Comparative Sociology,* 10 (Mar.-June 1969): 95-116.

_____. "Technology and Social Behavior of Workers in Four Countries: A Socio-Technical Perspective." *American Sociological Review,* 37 (Dec. 1972): 727-38.

Frankel, Charles. *The Democratic Prospect.* New York: Harper and Row, 1964.

Franklin, Jack L., and Joseph E. Scott. "Parental Values: An Inquiry into Occupational Setting." *Journal of Marriage and the Family,* 32 (Aug. 1970): 406-9.

Freedman, Ronald, and Deborah Freedman. "Farm-Reared Elements in the Nonfarm Population." *Rural Sociology,* 21, 1-4 (1956): 50-61.

Frenkel-Brunswik, Else. "The Interaction of Psychological and Sociological Factors in Political Behavior." *American Political Science Review,* 46 (Mar. 1952): 44-65.

Furstenberg, Jr., Frank F. "Industrialization and the American Family: A Look Backward." *American Sociological Review,* 31 (June 1966): 327-37.

Gawthrop, Louis C., ed. *The Administrative Process and Democratic Theory.* Boston: Houghton-Mifflin, 1970.

Germani, Gino. "The Social and Political Consequences of Mobility." In *Economic Development,* edited by S.M. Lipset and N.J. Smelser. Chicago: Aldine, 1966.

Gilbert, Claire. *Community Power Structure.* Gainesville, Fla.: Univ. of Florida Press, 1972.

Goffman, Erving. "The Mortification of Self." In *Conformity, Resistance and Self-Determination: The Individual and Authority,* edited by R. Flacks. Boston: Little, Brown, 1973.

Goldthorpe, John H. et al. *The Affluent Worker: Industrial Attitudes and Behavior.* London: Cambridge Univ. Press, 1968.

_____. *The Affluent Worker: Political Attitudes and Behavior.* London: Cambridge Univ. Press, 1968.

Goodman, Paul. *Growing Up Absurd: Problems of Youth in the Organized System.* New York: Random House, 1960.

Goslin, David A., ed. *Handbook of Socialization Theory and Research.* Chicago: Rand McNally, 1971.

Greenfield, Sidney M. "Industrialization and the Family in Sociological Theory." *American Journal of Sociology,* 67 (Nov. 1961): 312-22.

Hall, Richard H. *Organizations: Structure and Process.* Englewood Cliffs, N.J.: Prentice-Hall, 1972.

Hamilton, Richard F. "Skill Level and Politics." *Public Opinion Quarterly,* 31 (Winter 1967): 390-99.

Hart, Vivian. *Distrust and Democracy.* London: Cambridge Univ. Press, 1978.

Harvey, Edward. "Technology and the Structure of Organizations." *American Sociological Review* (Apr. 1968): 247-59.

"Have Americans Lost Faith in the Political System?" Ann Arbor, Mich., *Institute for Social Research Newsletter*, 1, 18 (Spring-Summer 1973).

Hayden, Tom. "The Port Huron Statement of Students for a Democratic Society." In *Directions in American Political Thought*, edited by K.M. Dolbeare, New York: Wiley, 1969.

Henry, Jules. *Culture Against Man.* New York: Random House, 1963.

Himmelstrand, Ulf. *Social Pressures, Attitudes, and Democratic Processes.* Stockholm, Sweden: Almquist and Wiksell, 1960.

Hobart, Charles F. "Commitment, Value Conflict and the Future of the American Family." *Marriage and Family Living* (Nov. 1963): 405-12.

Hunt, David. *Parents and Children in History.* New York: Basic Books, 1970.

"Inevitable Hierarchical Gap Emerges in Study of Capitalist and Socialist Organizations." Ann Arbor, Mich., *Institute for Social Research Newsletter,* 2, 3 (Autumn 1974): 4-5.

Inkeles, Alex. "Industrial Man: The Relation of Status to Experience, Perception, and Value." *American Journal of Sociology,* 66 (July 1960): 1-31.

_____. "Making Men Modern: On the Causes and Consequences of Individual Change in Six Developing Countries." *American Journal of Sociology,* 75, 2 (Sept. 1969): 208-25.

_____. "Participant Citizenship in Six Developing Countries." *American Political Science Review,* 63 (Dec. 1969): 1120-41.

Jaros, Dean. *Socialization to Politics.* New York: Praeger, 1973.

Jaros, Dean; Herbert Hirsch; and Frederick J. Fleron, Jr. "The Malevolent Leader: Political Socialization in an American Sub-culture." In *The Learning of Political Behavior*, edited by N. Adler and C. Harrington. Glenview, Ill.: Scott, Foresman, 1970.

Jay, Antony. "Corporation Man." Reprinted in *Intellectual Digest* (Feb. 1972): 69-76.

Johnson, Richard T., and William G. Ouchi. "Made in America (under Japanese management)." *Harvard Business Review,* 52 (Sept.-Oct. 1974): 61-69.

Kagan, Jerome. *Personality Development.* New York: Harcourt Brace Jovanovich, 1971.

Kahn, Robert L. "The Meaning of Work: Interpretation and Proposals for Measurement." In *The Human Meaning of Social Change,* edited by A. Campbell and P. Converse. New York: Russell Sage Foundation, 1972.

Kariel, Henry S., ed. *Frontiers of Democratic Theory.* New York: Random House, 1970.

Kasarda, John D., and Morris Janowitz. "Community Attachment in Mass Society." *American Sociological Review,* 39, 3 (June 1974): 328-39.

Katz, Michael B. *Class, Bureaucracy and Schools.* New York: Praeger, 1971.

Kaufman, Herbert. "Administrative Decentralization and Political Power." In *The Dimensions of Public Administration: Introductory Readings,* edited by J.A. Uveges, Jr. Boston: Holbrook Press, 1971.

Kerr, Clark, et al. *Industrialism and Industrial Man.* Cambridge: Harvard Univ. Press, 1960.

Kilpatrick, Franklin P., et al. *The Image of the Federal Service.* Washington, D.C.: Brookings Institution, 1964.

_____. *Source Book of a Study of Occupational Values and the Image of the Federal Service.* Washington, D.C.: Brookings Institution, 1964.

King, Edward L. "How the Army Destroyed Itself." *Saturday Review* (May 6, 1972): 29-33.

Knutson, Jeanne N., ed. *Handbook of Political Psychology.* San Francisco: Jossey-Bass, 1973.

_____. "Personality in the Study of Politics." In *Handbook of Political Psychology,* edited by Jeanne N. Knutson. San Francisco: Jossey-Bass, 1973.

Kohn, Melvin L. "Bureaucratic Man: A Portrait and an Interpretation." *American Sociological Review,* 36 (June 1971): 461-74.

_____. *Class and Conformity.* Homewood, Ill.: Dorsey, 1969.

Kornhauser, Arthur W., with Otto M. Reid. *Mental Health of the Industrial Worker.* New York: Wiley, 1965.

Kornhauser, William. *The Politics of Mass Society.* Glencoe, Ill.: Free Press, 1959.

Kramer, Daniel C. *Participatory Democracy*. New York: General Learning Press, 1972.

Kramer, Ralph M. *Participation of the Poor*. Englewood Cliffs, N.J.: Prentice-Hall, 1969.

Lantz, Herman R., et al. "Pre-Industrial Patterns in the Colonial Family in America: A Content Analysis of Colonial Magazines." *American Sociological Review*, 33 (June 1968): 413-426.

Lantz, Herman R.; Jane Keyes; and Martin Schultz. "The American Family in the Preindustrial Period: From Base Lines in History to Change." *American Sociological Review*, 40 (Feb. 1975): 21-36.

Lantz, Herman; Martin Schultz; and Mary O'Hara. "The Changing American Family from the Preindustrial to the Industrial Period: A Final Report." *American Sociological Review*, 42 (June 1977): 406-21.

Laslett, Barbara. "Social Change and the Family: Los Angeles, California, 1850-1870." *American Sociological Review*, 42 (Apr. 1977): 268-91.

Lasswell, Harold. *Psychopathology and Politics*. Chicago: Univ. of Chicago Press, 1930.

Laumann, Edward O. *Bonds of Pluralism: The Form and Substance of Urban Social Networks*. New York: Wiley, 1973.

Lipset, Seymour M. *Political Man*. Garden City, N.Y.: Doubleday, 1960.

Lipsitz, Lewis. "Work Life and Political Attitudes: A Study of Manual Workers." *American Political Science Review*, 58, 4 (Dec. 1964): 951-62.

Litwak, Eugene. "Occupational Mobility and Extended Family Cohesion." *American Sociological Review*, 25 (Feb. 1960): 9-23.

Lowi, Theodore J. *The End of Liberalism*. New York: Norton, 1969.
_____. *The Politics of Disorder*. New York: Basic Books, 1971.

Lynd, Staughton. "The Movement: A New Beginning." In *The Case for Participatory Democracy*, edited by C.G. Benello and D. Roussopoulos. New York: Viking Press, 1971.

MacFarland, Andres. *Power and Leadership in Pluralist Systems*. Stanford, Calif.: Stanford Univ. Press, 1969.

MacKinnon, Frank. *Posture and Politics*. Toronto: Univ. of Toronto Press, 1973.

March, James G., and Herbert Simon, with Harold Guetzkow. *Organizations.* New York: Wiley, 1958.

Marcuse, Herbert. *One Dimensional Man.* Boston: Beacon, 1966.

Maslow, Abraham H. *Toward a Psychology of Being.* New York: Van Nostrand Reinhold, 1968.

Massialas, Byron G. *Political Youth, Traditional Schools.* Englewood Cliffs, N.J.: Prentice-Hall, 1972.

Matthews, Donald R., and James W. Prothro. *Negroes and the New Southern Politics.* New York: Harcourt, Brace, 1962.

Mayntz, Renate. "Citizen Participation in Germany: Nature and Extent." Paper prepared for the 5th World Congress of the International Political Science Assn., Paris, Sept. 1961.

McCandless, Naya N. "Childhood Socialization." In *Handbook of Socialization Theory and Research,* edited by D.A. Goslin. Chicago: Rand McNally, 1971.

McClelland, David C. *The Achieving Society.* Princeton, N.J.: Van Nostrand, 1961.

McDermott, John. "Technology: The Opiate of the Intellectuals." Special supplement, *New York Times,* July 31, 1969, pp. 25-35.

McKinley, D.G. *Social Class and Family Life.* New York: Free Press, 1964.

Medvedev, Zhores. "The Medvedev Papers." *Intellectual Digest* (Oct. 1971): 61-68.

Meissner, Martin. "The Long Arm of the Job: A Study of Work and Leisure." *Industrial Relations,* 10 (Oct. 1971): 239-60.

_____. *Technology and the Worker.* San Francisco: Chandler, 1969.

Myer, Marshall W. *Bureaucratic Structure and Authority.* New York: Harper and Row, 1972.

Michels, Robert. *Political Parties: A Sociological Study of Oligarchical Tendencies of Modern Democracy.* New York: Collier, 1962.

Milbreth, Lester W. *Political Participation.* Chicago: Rand McNally, 1965.

_____. "Political Participation in the States." In *Comparative State Politics,* edited by H. Jacob and K. Vines. Boston: Little, Brown, 1965.

Milbreth, Lester W., and Walter Klein. "Personality Correlates of Political Participation." *Acta Sociologica,* 6 (Fasc. 1-2, 1962): 53-66.

Mill, J.S. *Considerations on Representative Government.* New York: Holt, Rinehart and Winston, 1973.

Miller, Daniel R., and Guy E. Swanson. *The Changing American Parent.* New York: Wiley, 1958.

Miller, George A., and Wesley Wager. "Adult Socialization, Organizational Structure, and Role Orientations." *Administrative Science Quarterly,* 16 (June 1971): 151-63.

Miller, S.M., and Martin Rein. "Participation, Poverty, and Administration." *Public Administration Review,* 29 (Jan./Feb. 1969): 15-25.

Mills, C. Wright. *White Collar.* New York: Oxford Univ. Press, 1951.

Miner, John B. "Changes in Student Attitudes toward Bureaucratic Prescriptions." *Administrative Science Quarterly.* 16, 3 (Sept. 1971).

Modell, John, and Tamara K. Hareven. "Urbanization and the Malleable Household: An Examination of Boarding and Lodging in American Families." *Journal of Marriage and the Family* (Aug. 1973): 467-69.

Moore, Wilbert E. "Occupational Socialization." In *Handbook of Socialization Theory and Research,* edited by D.A. Goslin. Chicago: Rand McNally, 1971.

Morris, David, and Karl Hess. *Neighborhood Power.* Boston: Beacon Press, 1975.

Mott, Paul E.; Floyd C. Mann; Quin McLaughlin; and Donald P. Warwick. *Shift Work.* Ann Arbor: Univ. of Michigan Press, 1965.

Myrdal, Gunnar. *Beyond the Welfare State.* New York: Bantam Books, 1971.

Neill, A.S. *Summerhill.* New York: Hart, 1960.

Neimi, Richard G. "Political Socialization." In *Handbook of Political Psychology,* edited by J.N. Knutson. San Francisco: Jossey-Bass, 1973.

Nettl, John P. *Political Mobilization: A Sociological Analysis of Methods and Concepts.* London: Farber, 1967.

Nie, Norma H.; G.B. Powell, Jr.; and K. Prewitt. "Social Structure and Political Participation: Developmental Relationships." In *Cross-National Micro-Analysis,* edited by J.C. Pierce and R.A. Pride. Beverly Hills: Sage Pubns., 1972.

Norton, Susan L. "Marital Migration in Essex County, Massachusetts, in the Colonial and Early Federal Periods." *Journal of Marriage and the Family* (Aug. 1973): 406-18.

Pahl, J.M., and R.E. Pahl. *Managers and Their Wives.* London: Allen Lane, 1971.

Parenti, Michael. *Power and the Powerless.* New York: St. Martin's Press, 1978.

Pateman, Carole. *Participation and Democratic Theory.* London: Cambridge Univ. Press, 1970.

Pavalko, Ronald M. *Sociology of Occupations and Professions.* Itasca, Ill.: Peacock, 1971.

Piven, Francis F., and Richard A. Cloward. *Regulating the Poor.* New York: Pantheon, 1971.

Porter, Lyman. "Job Attitudes in Management: Perceived Deficiencies in Need Fulfillment as a Function of Size of Company." *Journal of Applied Psychology,* 46, 6 (Dec. 1962): 375-84.

_____. "Job Attitudes in Management: Perceived Deficiencies in Need Fulfillment as a Function of Size of Company." *Journal of Applied Psychology,* 47, 6 (1963): 386-97.

Porter, Lyman, and Edward Lawler. "Properties of Organization Structure in Relation to Job Behavior." In *Readings in Organizational Behavior and Human Performance,* edited by L.L. Cummings and W.E. Scott, Jr. Homewood, Ill.: Irwin, Dorsey, 1969.

Pranger, Robert J. *The Eclipse of Citizenship: Power and Participation in Contemporary Politics.* New York: Holt, Rinehart and Winston, 1968.

Prewitt, Kenneth, and Alan Stone. *The Ruling Elites.* New York: Harper and Row, 1973.

Reich, Charles. *The Greening of America.* New York: Bantam Books, 1971.

Renshon, Stanley A. *Psychological Needs and Political Behavior: A Theory of Personality and Political Efficacy.* New York: Free Press, 1977.

Ricci, David. *Community Power and Democratic Theory: The Logic of Political Analysis.* New York: Random House, 1971.

Richardson, Bradley M. *The Political Culture of Japan.* Berkeley: Univ. of California Press, 1974.

Riley, Matilda W., et al. "Socialization for the Middle and Later Years." In *Handbook of Socialization Theory and Research,* edited by D.A. Goslin. Chicago: Rand McNally, 1971.

Rokkan, Stein. "Approaches to the Study of Political Participation." *Acta Sociologica,* 6 (Fasc. 1-2, 1962): 1-8.

————. "The Comparative Study of Political Participation: Notes toward a Perspective on Current Research." In *Essays on the Behavioral Study of Politics,* edited by A. Ranney. Urbana: Univ. of Illinois Press, 1962.

Roszak, Theodore. *Where the Wasteland Ends.* New York: Doubleday, 1972.

Scanzoni, John H. *Opportunity and the Family.* New York: Free Press, 1970.

Schumpeter, Joseph A. *Capitalism, Socialism and Democracy,* 3d ed. New York: Harper and Row, 1962.

Sennett, Richard. *Families Against the City.* Cambridge: Harvard Univ. Press, 1970.

Shepard, Jon M. *Organizational Issues in Industrial Society.* Englewood Cliffs, N.J.: Prentice-Hall, 1972.

Sheppard, Harold L., and Neal Q. Harrick. *Where Have All the Robots Gone?* New York: Free Press, 1972.

Shklar, Judith N. *Men and Citizens: Rousseau's Social Theory.* London: Cambridge Univ. Press, 1969.

Shorter, Edward, ed. *Work and Community in the West.* New York: Harper and Row, 1973.

Skolnick, Arlene. "Personality Correlates and Antecedents of Kin Involvement." Paper presented to the Annual Meeting of the American Sociological Assn., 1975.

————. *The Intimate Environment.* Boston: Little, Brown, 1973.

Skolnick, Arlene, and Jerome H. Skolnick. *Intimacy, Family, and Society.* Boston: Little, Brown, 1974.

Smith, Daniel S. "Parental Power and Marriage Patterns: An Analysis of Historical Trends in Hingham, Massachusetts." *Journal of Marriage and the Family* (Aug. 1973): 419-28.

Stenberg, Carl W. "The History and Future of Citizen Participation: An Overview." Address to the National Conference on Public Administration, Denver, Colo., Apr. 19, 1971.

Sussman, Marvin B. "The Help Pattern in the Middle-Class Family." *American Sociological Review,* 18 (Feb. 1953): 22-28.

———. "The Isolated Nuclear Family: Fact or Fiction?" *Social Problems,* 6 (Spring 1959): 333-40.

Tannenbaum, Arnold S., et al. *Hierarchy in Organizations.* San Francisco: Jossey-Bass, 1974.

Thompson, Dennis F. *The Democratic Citizen.* London: Cambridge Univ. Press, 1970.

Townsend, James. *Political Participation in Communist China.* Berkeley: Univ. of California Press, 1967.

Tudor, Bill. "A Specification of Relationships Between Job Complexity and Powerlessness." *American Sociological Review,* 37 (Oct. 1972): 596-604.

U.S., Department of Health, Education and Welfare. *Work in America,* Report of a Special Task Force to the Secretary of Health, Education and Welfare. Cambridge: M.I.T. Press, 1973.

Verba, Sidney. *Small Groups and Political Behavior: A Study of Leadership.* Princeton, N.J.: Princeton Univ. Press, 1961.

Verba, Sidney, and Norman H. Nie. *Participation in America: Political Democracy and Social Equality.* New York: Harper and Row, 1972.

Verba, Sidney; Norman H. Nie; and Jae-On Kim. *The Modes of Democratic Participation: A Cross-National Comparison.* Beverly Hills: Sage, 1971.

Walker, Jack. "A Critique of the Elitist Theory of Democracy." *American Political Science Review,* 60 (June 1966): 285.

Wheeler, Harvey. *Democracy in a Revolutionary Era.* Santa Barbara, Calif.: Center for the Study of Democratic Institutions, 1970.

Whyte, W.H. *The Organization Man.* New York: Simon and Schuster, 1956.

Wilcox, Herbert G. "The Culture Trait of Hierarchy in Middle Class Children." *Public Administration Review* (May/June 1968): 222-33.

———. "Hierarchy, Human Nature, and the Participative Panacea." *Public Administration Review,* 29 (Jan./Feb. 1969): 53-63.

Wilensky, Harold L. "Work, Careers, and Social Integration." Bobbs-Merrill reprint from *International Social Science Journal,* 7 (Fall 1960).

Wilson, James Q. "The Bureaucracy Problem." *The Public Interest* 6 (Winter 1967): 3-9.

Wilson, James Q., and Edward C. Banfield. "Public Regardingness as a Value Premise in Voting Behavior." *American Political Science Review,* 57, 4 (Dec. 1964): 876-87.

"Women in Work—Facts and Fictions." Ann Arbor, Mich., *Institute for Social Research Newsletter,* 1, 16 (Autumn 1972).

Woodcock, George. "Democracy, Heretical and Radical." In *The Case for Participatory Democracy,* edited by C.G. Benello and D. Roussopoulos. New York: Viking Press, 1971.

Woodward, Julian, and Elmo Roper. "Political Activity of American Citizens." *American Political Science Review,* 44 (Dec. 1950): 872-85.

Yam, Tuneo, and Hisaya Nonoyama. "Isolation of the Nuclear Family and Kinship Organization in Japan: A Hypothetical Approach to the Relationships Between the Family and Society." *Journal of Marriage and the Family* (Nov. 1967): 783-96.

Young, Michael, and Peter Willmott. *The Symmetrical Family.* New York: Pantheon, 1973.

Zaretsky, Eli. *Capitalism, the Family, and Personal Life.* New York: Harper and Row, 1976.

Index

205